Dr Melanie Fennell is a clinical psychologist and an internationally recognised expert on low self-esteem. As well as being one of the first clinician researchers to introduce cognitive therapy to the UK, she was a founder member of the Oxford Cognitive Therapy Centre (OCTC), an internationally recognised centre of excellence in cognitive therapy and training.

She has also worked as a researcher at Oxford University Department of Psychiatry for a number of years, contributing to the development of psychological treatment for a wide range of emotional problems. In addition to seeing patients, she runs many workshops and presents research papers at major international cognitive conferences on low self-esteem.

She is the author of the bestselling *Overcoming Low Self-Esteem*.

Boost Your Confidence

Improving self-esteem step-by-step

Melanie Fennell

ROBINSON

With gratitude for the wisdom and courage of the
patients I have had the privilege of working with
over the years; for the inspiration and support of
dear colleagues; for loved family and friends and
(last but not least) for Sally.

Constable & Robinson Ltd
3 The Lanchesters
162 Fulham Palace Road
London W6 9ER
www.constablerobinson.com

First published in the UK by Robinson,
an imprint of Constable & Robinson Ltd, 2011

A copy of the British Library Cataloguing in
Publication Data is available from the British Library

ISBN: 978-1-84901-400-7

Important note
This book is not intended as a substitute for medical advice or treatment.
Any person with a condition requiring medical attention should consult
a qualified medical practitioner or suitable therapist.

Printed and bound in the EU

1 3 5 7 9 10 8 6 4 2

CONTENTS

CONTENTS

1

WHY CONFIDENCE MATTERS

Do you have a secret vision of the life you feel you should be living? Perhaps you see yourself in a loving, supportive relationship with someone who brings out the best in you. Or maybe you dream of bounding out of bed in the morning, fired by enthusiasm for a job or vocation you're passionate about. Perhaps you simply picture a slimmer, fitter and healthier version of yourself, with energy to spare.

You might already have a theory about why your dream life remains tantalisingly out of reach. Perhaps you tell yourself it's unrealistic, and that circumstances, bad luck or lack of opportunity will always work against you. But maybe you also have a feeling that there is something inside you that's holding you back, a quality that you can't quite put your finger on, but that you know is there. Do you ever wonder whether there's something about the way you *are* that's influencing the way your life is shaping up? If so, your instincts could be right. There *is* something deep inside all of us that has a powerful effect on every aspect of our daily life. It's called self-confidence.

Think of a self-confident person you know or have met in the past. What is it that you admire about them? Do they make an instant impact when they walk into a room? Do they have an in-built resilience to life's ups and downs, and see problems as challenges to learn from? Are they excited by new experiences and adventures? Or perhaps they radiate natural warmth, genuineness and openness?

It's true that self-confidence allows you to push the boundaries and live a big life. But being self-confident is not about being an extrovert, or the life and soul of every party. It's not about thinking you're the most fantastic thing since sliced bread. It's about simply feeling happy in your own skin. Inner self-confidence is like being your own best friend and cheerleading team rolled into one – it allows you to treat yourself with kindness and compassion, and instinctively act in your own best interests. It helps you enhance the lives of those around you, by being the best partner, friend and parent that you can be. It allows you to maximise the opportunities that come your way, and fulfil your true potential.

If you've picked up this book, chances are you already have an inkling that lack of self-confidence is affecting your life. Perhaps you've asked yourself the following questions.

• Why don't my relationships work out?

Do you wonder why you're still single, long after all your friends have settled down? Do new relationships never live up to their initial potential? Or are you stuck in a destructive relationship – or pattern of relationships – that you can't seem to get out of? Do you feel crushed by criticism and disapproval, and can't bear the thought of anyone disliking you? Do you sometimes feel that friends and colleagues take advantage, because they know you won't complain? Do you feel uncomfortably self-conscious in a group of people you don't know well? Do your friendships tend to get stuck at a small-talk level? Or perhaps you have an urge to please everyone, and feel that if you're not the life and soul of every party, people won't want to know you?

> *Meena grew up thinking she was inferior to other people, and had nothing worthwhile to say. Now as an adult, she has a pattern of falling for self-centred men who demand a lot of attention from Meena, but give her little in return.*

- Why is my career going nowhere?

Are you frustrated, bored, under-appreciated, over-worked or underpaid in your job? Do you have a nagging fear of failure that never leaves you? Do you find it hard to feel satisfied or pleased with what you've achieved, and to recognise your efforts or talents, even though you put in 110 per cent? Or do you have a feeling that you're not quite reaching your full potential, and that you could, and should, be doing more? Are you aware of avoiding challenges and situations that take you out of your comfort zone? Is there something you'd love to learn or explore, but somehow, never get round to doing, in case you're no good at it?

> *Kevin struggled at school due to undiagnosed dyslexia and grew up believing he was 'stupid'. He's been in the same unchallenging job for years, and refuses his manager's suggestion of going for promotion, because he's convinced they'll find out how 'stupid' he really is.*

- Why can't I lose weight?

Is your wardrobe full of clothes you can't fit into any more? Would you dress differently if you were slimmer? Do you avoid social events because you feel so fat and unattractive? Do your best intentions to eat a healthy, balanced diet inevitably fall by the wayside? Do you drink more than you know you should, smoke or take recreational drugs, even though you're well aware that it's bad for you? Do you struggle with low energy levels or seem to have one health problem after another? Do you rarely take a day off or ask for help when you're ill? Do you find it hard to treat yourself or take time to relax?

Nicki was an energetic, sporty child but, by eighteen, she was very overweight. She's now been yo-yo dieting for more than fifteen years. How she feels about herself depends on what the scales say in the morning, and what she has and hasn't eaten throughout the day.

WHAT IS HEALTHY SELF-CONFIDENCE?

You don't have to be an extra special person to have healthy self-confidence – lots of normal, average people have it. Healthy self-confidence doesn't mean thinking you're great at everything. It's about accepting yourself for who you are, faults and weaknesses included, and living a life that's in line with your values and what's important to you. If you have healthy self-confidence, you'll . . .

- Want to be accepted and liked by the people you care about, but won't expect every single person you meet to like you.
- Feel open about expressing your needs and emotions

in relationships, and be able to both ask for and give help when needed.

- Know that negative emotions like hurt and anxiety are unavoidable in life, but have the tools to cope with them and learn from them.
- Set realistic, flexible goals for yourself and enjoy the journey of discovery as much as the achievement itself.
- Take care of yourself and make time for rest, relaxation and enjoyment without feeling guilty.

CAN PEOPLE REALLY CHANGE?

Yes, and we have proof, thanks to advances in neuroscience. Brain-imaging techniques have shown that changing the way you think and act can not only change the way you feel about yourself, but actually changes the structure of the brain. Scientists call this phenomenon 'neural plasticity'. So although changing your behaviour and thinking habits can feel artificial and like hard work at first, take heart – it will feel more natural as time goes by.

HOW THIS BOOK CAN HELP

By reading this book, you're opening the door to the possibility of a different future.

In this book you will . . .

- Start to understand what knocked your natural self-confidence in the first place, however long ago that was.
- Discover how low self-confidence can create its own vicious circle, making you think and act in a way that

stops your natural self-confidence from ever fully recovering and developing.

- Learn that being compassionate to yourself has a big role to play in building self-confidence, and how it can help you develop a new objective viewpoint of who you are – one that's more realistic, and helpful.
- Embrace your talents and strong points, and put your flaws and weaknesses into perspective.

The truly amazing thing is you don't even have to be fully convinced that this book will revolutionise your life and make a new person of you for it to help. You just need to be open-minded, curious about how your own mind works, and willing to invest time in finding out where your poor self-confidence came from, and how it's affecting your life. You need to take the plunge, throw yourself in the deep end and immerse yourself in the book – simply sitting on the side, dipping in your toes won't bring the same results!

So just reading isn't enough – you need to do your homework! That means making notes, filling in the work-sheets and carrying out the practical exercises. Stick with it, and you'll start to undermine old, negative beliefs about yourself, however entrenched they may be. You'll start to become aware of self-limiting patterns of thinking and acting. You'll also work out – and put to the test – more helpful and realistic alternatives to your old habits.

The book is based on a form of psychotherapy known as 'Cognitive Behaviour Therapy' – or CBT. It's been much talked about in recent years so there's a good chance you've already heard about it. But it's not just the latest self-help fad – CBT has been around since the 1960s, long enough for thousands of psychologists and other mental health professionals all over the world to be convinced that it works. Unlike some talking therapies, CBT takes a very practical, down-to-earth approach. Emotions, motivations, thoughts and feelings can be intangible, but CBT helps you pin them down, and really understand where they came from, and what keeps them alive.

CBT was originally developed as a treatment for depression by an American psychiatrist, Professor Aaron T. Beck. It's now used successfully to help people deal with a much wider range of problems, including phobias, stress, shyness, eating disorders, panic attacks, drug and alcohol misuse – and, of course, self-confidence.

With CBT, you can make small but meaningful changes within days. It works because it's interactive – you take a very active role, putting new ideas into practice on a day-to-day basis and experimenting with acting differently. This means you experience the impact of change for yourself, so it's more likely to have an effect. Taking a long, hard and objective look at yourself can be challenging, but CBT guides you through practical, step-by-step exercises that make it easier. As well as understanding yourself in new ways, it may leave you with a more questioning approach to life in general – CBT encourages you to question your thoughts, self-beliefs and self-image. But as it's solution-focused, the aim is not to simply uncover old wounds, but to teach you how to heal them.

Changing how you think and act from moment to moment can have an immediate effect on how you see yourself. But it's more than just a quick fix. CBT teaches you skills that you will rely on for the rest of your life.

QUIZ: HOW'S YOUR SELF-CONFIDENCE?

Take a look at the following ten questions. Next to each statement, put a tick in the column that best reflects how you feel about yourself. Be honest – there are no right or wrong answers here, simply the truth about how you see yourself. Then count up the number of A, B and C answers.

How's your self-confidence?	A – Yes, most of the time	B – Yes, some-times	C – No, very rarely
1 I tend to be compassionate and encouraging towards myself, rather than self-critical.			
2 I generally have a good opinion of myself.			
3 I think it's right that good things and pleasure are a part of my life.			
4 I like myself.			
5 I can list my strengths, skills and good points just as easily as my flaws and weaknesses.			
6 I feel good about myself.			
7 I feel I deserve other people's attention and time.			

8 Health and wellbeing are important to me and I make an effort to look after myself properly.			
9 I judge myself by the same standards that I apply to other people.			
10 On the whole, my experience of life so far has taught me to value and appreciate myself.			

Scoring

Mainly 'A's: Congratulations! If you've answered honestly, you have the gift of self-confidence. You are generally comfortable in accepting yourself as you are and your self-respect is likely to be reflected in the way you live – you'll have healthy relationships, will prioritise taking care of yourself, and make sure there's enough time for fun and relaxation, no matter how busy life gets. You're not blind to your weaknesses, but you know that you have intrinsic value and worth as a human being. But that doesn't mean this book isn't for you! Even the most self-confident people experience occasional moments of self-doubt (for example, at a job interview or on a first date). It's worth reading on for ideas on overcoming occasional nerves or feelings of apprehension, and ensuring your self-confidence remains robust, whatever challenges you may face in the future.

Mainly 'B's: You have a generally realistic perspective on yourself, and can cope with life's ups and downs by talking through your feelings with a good friend, partner or close family member, or by dusting yourself down and picking yourself up. But you may find that in certain situations – whether related to work, relationships or your social life – your confidence deserts you and you begin to feel anxious or self-critical. You may have used avoidance tactics to cope with this in the past. Are you terrified by meetings or at the thought of presenting your ideas to your boss? Do you avoid seeking promotion or a new job because you can't face interviews? Are you great at one-to-ones, but hate socialising in a crowd? Or are you happy to be one of the gang, but experience stumbling blocks that stop you from building a long-term, one-to-one relationship? Are you successful and well-loved, but feel like you've failed in life because you're not your ideal weight? Working through this book will help uncover the source of these elements of self-doubt and highlight the thoughts and behaviour that feed into them. You'll also learn how to build a new perspective that will help you overcome your stumbling blocks.

Mainly 'C's: Well done for picking up this book – you now have the power to change your life in your hands. Your answers suggest that lack of self-confidence is already having a limiting effect on your life. You have an inner conviction that deep down, you're somehow lacking or inadequate. You probably have a very vocal inner critic, or carry round feelings of guilt at generally not being good enough. You are troubled by uncertainty and self-doubt, and when things go wrong you blame yourself. You're harder on yourself than you'd ever be on other people in your life, and have difficulty in feeling that you have any true worth, or that you deserve to treat yourself with respect and kindness. You may find it hard to get really close to other people. Perhaps you've always felt this way, or came to feel like this after a major event such as a bereavement, the ending of a relationship, the loss of a job, or other life changes such as becoming a mother, or experiencing severe stress or illness. Indeed, you may have experienced serious psychological health problems such as problem drinking, eating disorders, depression or suicidal thinking. But it's gone on long enough and, deep down, you know that something has to change. This book is here to help you understand why you feel the way you do, and show you the changes you need to make to feel differently. You've found your way to the right door to greater contentment – are you ready to step through?

IMPROVE YOUR SELF-CONFIDENCE, CHANGE YOUR LIFE

Here are just some of the ways you may benefit from taking the time and effort to improve your self-confidence.

- You'll meet challenges head-on. You may feel mildly apprehensive in a challenging situation, but you won't have any trouble managing the apprehension. You'll find it easy to reassure yourself.
- You'll have a sense of perspective. You'll see difficulties in life as problems to be solved, rather than a sign that there is something fundamentally wrong with you as a person.
- You'll have the ability to both recognise and answer self-critical thoughts and to be kind and compassionate to yourself, especially when times are tough.
- You'll find it easier to relate to other people, and feel comfortable about asking for help.
- You'll have a more balanced self-image and come to

accept and appreciate yourself, fully, warts and all, for who you really are.

- You'll have more respect for your personal strengths, abilities and skills.
- You'll have a feeling of self-worth and feel entitled to a happy life.

WHAT CAUSES LOW SELF-CONFIDENCE?

You'll explore in detail the reasons behind your own low self-confidence throughout the book. But in general, the causes of poor self-confidence come into three main categories . . .

- Incidents in the past, such as childhood bullying or a difficult relationship with a parent.
- Aspects of your current life, such as problems in a close personal relationship, workplace pressures or conflicts, or just ongoing stress.
- A side-effect of another psychological health issue, such as depression, anxiety or panic attacks.

Low self-confidence or depression?

Sometimes low self-confidence is a side-effect of clinical depression, a condition which requires treatment in its own right. Consult your GP if you have experienced five or more of the following symptoms for at least two weeks:

☐ consistently low mood, or feeling 'empty'

☐ loss of enjoyment or interest in things that normally give you pleasure

☐ changes in your appetite or weight

☐ changes to your sleep

☐ restlessness, or else feeling like you've gone into slow motion, so much so that others have noticed

☐ feeling tired all the time

☐ feeling guilty or worthless

☐ finding it hard to concentrate or make decisions

☐ thoughts about death or suicide

If you recognise these symptoms, seeking treatment may well also restore your self-confidence, because negative thoughts about yourself are a key feature of depression. Nonetheless, the ideas in this book may still be useful to you – research shows that low self-confidence can make people vulnerable to becoming depressed. If you feel a bit daunted by the prospect, try focusing on Chapters 5, 6 and 7. They deal with silencing self-critical thoughts and focusing on positive aspects of yourself, which may strike a chord with you.

Ten top tips for getting the most out of this book

1 View it as a project. Set aside 20 to 30 minutes every day for the next month to read, reflect, and complete the exercises. It's a big commitment, particularly as it may be hard going at times, when you're uncovering issues that feel painful or uncomfortable. But it's a commitment that could have a life-changing pay-off.

2 Have a sheet of paper or a notebook by you and note down anything that occurs to you as you read – ideas, memories, hunches.

3   Try to keep an open mind, and approach the ideas and techniques you will find in the book in a spirit of curiosity. What might there be for you to discover? How can you apply what you read in your own life? Think of yourself as an explorer, investigating the territory of your own mind.

4   Take part. If you really want to make changes in how you feel about yourself, it's important to realise that reading and rethinking are only part of the story. The best way to change things is to be willing to experiment with new ideas and skills in everyday life. Direct experience is the best teacher.

5   Work in a way that suits you. Some people prefer to skim-read the whole book first, or glance at each chapter heading, before working through the book systematically.

6   Keep notes. As you go, you will find various worksheets designed to help you to notice, question and test old patterns of thought. Many people find these sheets helpful in providing a sort of framework for their investigations – filling them in helps to keep things on track, and remind you of the changes you want to make. Just doing the work in your head, or perhaps keeping your own notebook or diary, may turn out to be all you need. Or why not experiment with the worksheets to see whether you find them useful?

7   Let it sink in. Resist the temptation to move on to the next chapter too soon. The ideas in the book build on each other so you'll get the best results if you take the time to understand each one properly before you move

on. Don't rush, or the ideas presented won't significantly affect the way you feel about yourself. There's no 'right' timeframe for completing the book – it might take a week, a month or six months. Go with what feels right for you.

8   Work with a friend. Some people are better suited to working in a team. If that's you, consider buying a copy for a friend and working through it chapter-by-chapter together, perhaps using email to discuss your insights and challenges. It can help you stay motivated and you may find an outside point of view helpful if you struggle to be objective about yourself.

9   Get the help you need. For some people, working through this book won't be enough and they may need help from a professionally trained counsellor or psychotherapist. This may be the case if you find focusing on your self-confidence is making you feel worse instead of better, or if your negative beliefs about yourself are so strong that you find it impossible to apply the ideas and practical skills suggested in the following chapters. Seeking psychological help is a wise and courageous thing to do, and nothing to be embarrassed about. Your doctor is a good starting point, or see pages 242–3 for a list of organisations that can help you find a qualified therapist. If you like the approach described in the book, your best bet might be to look for a cognitive behaviour therapist.

10 Chart your progress. Keep a note of your score from the *How's your self-confidence? quiz* you've just done, then retake the quiz at the end of book. You should end up with more 'A's and few, if any, 'C's.

Why this book works

The difference between this book and lots of other self-help books is that it's not about convincing yourself that you're fantastic, or amazing, or that you can do anything you set your mind to. It's simply about shifting the balance in the way you perceive yourself. It's not about pretending your faults and weaknesses don't exist, it's about accepting them as a part of yourself, along with your many strengths, talents and good qualities. By doing this, you can overcome the low self-confidence that has been hampering your ability to enjoy life to the full and achieve your true potential.

2

WHERE DOES YOUR
LOW SELF-CONFIDENCE
COME FROM?

This chapter is about discovering where your lack of self-confidence comes from. Here's a quick overview of what you'll learn. The heart of the matter is old beliefs about yourself, learned through experience, but which are no longer relevant or useful. These old beliefs boil down to something that in CBT terms we call your 'Bottom Line' – a view of yourself such as 'I am unimportant'. But it's not quite as simple as that. If you believe your Bottom Line is an accurate reflection of who you are, you will have had to develop certain strategies to help you get by and feel OK about yourself. These strategies are your Rules for Living. You may feel that your Rules protect and support you, but as you'll discover later in the book, they actually keep your low self-confidence going.

Here's how it works:

Experiences

↓

Your Bottom Line

↓

Your Rules for Living

THE POWER OF OLD BELIEFS

Did you grow up believing in Santa Claus? You had every reason to do so – after all, the people you trusted the most in the world, such as your parents and teachers, told you he existed. You even saw the 'evidence' with your own eyes at Christmas in the pile of presents he delivered. If you left a mince pie or glass of beer out for him, they'd be gone by morning, along with the carrots for the reindeer. It made perfect sense to change your behaviour based on this belief, by trying to be extra good in the days leading up to Christmas.

Now imagine growing up thinking you are a 'difficult and demanding' child and a lot of trouble for your parents. People you trust (parents and other family members) tell you it's true. You see the evidence – your mother shouting at you and often telling your father that you've been 'awful' all day. It would make perfect sense to try to change your behaviour by being quiet, less boisterous and more withdrawn, and trying to second-guess what people expect of you.

But a belief that you are 'difficult' is no more correct than believing in Santa Claus, even if it feels as real to you as Father Christmas does to a four-year-old. An outsider looking on may see a normal, lively, demanding child and a mother who is under a lot of stress and often overwhelmed. But given this situation, chances are that you'd grow up with a deeply held belief that somehow you're not really worth the bother.

In this chapter you will learn . . .

- What your own deeply held beliefs are and where they have come from.
- How your old beliefs have influenced the way you act and the decisions you've made.
- How, in turn, your actions and decisions have confirmed any negative beliefs, creating a vicious circle of low self-confidence.

Delving into the past can be hard, but it's the first step in letting go of these beliefs, finally accepting that they aren't true, and replacing them with something more accurate and more helpful. It's not about handing out blame or wallowing in self-pity, it's simply the first part of a fact-finding mission that will help you live the life you deserve.

The way you feel about yourself, the way you judge what's going on in your life from day to day, and how much you value yourself as a person – these are at the heart of self-confidence. Unless you challenge and replace your negative beliefs, there's not much chance of changing the way you feel about yourself, no matter how outwardly successful your life may be.

Tips for getting the most out of this chapter

- Keep a special notebook and write down the thoughts and feelings that come up.

- Stick with it – delving into unhappy memories is never easy, but if you want to make changes the first step is to understanding yourself better than you do now.

THE CYCLE OF LOW SELF-CONFIDENCE

First things first – your view of yourself is an opinion, not a fact, and there's a good chance that it's not very accurate. 'But I know myself better than anyone!' you may protest. Well, it's true that you may *feel* you know yourself better than anyone. But – since it's just an opinion – your view of yourself can be biased, exaggerated or just plain wrong. If you gave ten people the same set of facts about you – your relationships, personal characteristics, life history and achievements – chances are you'd get ten different 'opinions' of the sort of person you are. And you couldn't say one of them is 'the truth' – they're just different points of view.

The ultimate aim of this book is change – changing your point of view about yourself to one that is more accurate, supportive and helpful. And the first step in this is understanding. After all, your opinion of yourself didn't come out of the blue, you formed it as a result of your life experiences. By retracing your steps, and unravelling this process, you will see exactly how this happened, and will understand why it is that this point of view feels so convincing and believable to you.

In many cases, although not all, it is childhood experiences that have the biggest influence on the opinions we hold about ourselves. What you saw, heard and experienced not just in your family home, but also at school, with your friends and out in the world in general has helped to shape the way you think about yourself today.

HOW POOR SELF-CONFIDENCE DEVELOPS

There's no doubt that experiencing abuse and neglect as a child can leave people thinking badly of themselves as they grow up. But far less dramatic experiences can also have a long-term effect. You may have lived in a comfortable home and had plenty to eat, nice clothes and regular treats like holidays, outings, Christmas presents and birthday parties, but still received negative messages about yourself that have become part of your Bottom Line. You may even ask yourself why you have such trouble valuing yourself when nothing really bad happened in your childhood. You may feel guilty thinking you have a 'problem' when there are so many people worse off than you. But if you're interested enough to be reading this book, chances are that you know there is something about the way you feel and think that's preventing you from being wholly content with yourself and your life.

Here are some examples of common situations and experiences that can lead to low self-confidence.

You were the odd one out in your family

Were you the only non-sporty child in a family of fitness enthusiasts, or the only bookish or artistic type in a non-academic family? Did you grow up with a sense of being different, and of not quite fitting in, or being an outsider? This can leave children feeling that there's something about them that's just 'not normal'.

CHARLOTTE

Charlotte's parents were scientists and her two older brothers loved science too. But Charlotte's passion was for art. At school she was above average in everything, but her real talents were for drawing, painting and creating designs. Her parents never took her work seriously, and were upset when she took the subject to A-level – they said she was throwing away her chance of getting into a decent university and should regard her art as just a hobby. Well, Charlotte went on to study fashion design at a top college and got taken on by a well-known clothing manufacturer. But she's always felt that other people are cleverer than she is, and worries that people will think she's frivolous, that her job – much as she loves it – is a bit of a joke. She compensates by trying to meet other people's expectations in other areas of her life, and by her self-deprecating humour, in an attempt to head off the criticism and dismissive comments that she expects.

You struggled at school

Children and young people who stand out in some way from the group can be left out, and are often miserable at the thought of being different. Moving schools, or to an area with a different accent, having a different colour skin, coming from another culture, or just not being considered one of the cool kids can leave young people vulnerable to teasing or bullying.

KEVIN

Kevin had been a lively and happy toddler. He loved his first year at school, but then began to struggle with learning to read and write because, unknown to his parents or teachers, he had dyslexia. While the rest of the class seemed to race ahead, he just couldn't seem to get the hang of it. He started to fool around in lessons and became the class clown, since making everyone laugh made him feel better about being bottom of the class. The teachers at his overcrowded school began to lose patience with him, and his parents would tell him he was lazy and was never going to get anywhere in life. He left school at 16 and took the first job he was offered in a local packaging factory. Kevin is a reliable and popular staff member who does his job well, but despite encouragement from his boss, he refuses to apply for management positions because he's sure they'll find out his secret – that he's 'stupid'.

You didn't fit in at school

Peer pressure is a powerful force and a big influence in children's lives, particularly when they hit adolescence. At a time when you are naturally moving away from identifying with your parents, there's usually a strong need to conform with your peer group. And feeling that your peers consider you a 'loser', or that you're not on the 'A-list', can damage your self-confidence for ever.

NICKI

Nicki's parents had grown up just after the Second World War, when food was still rationed in the UK. To her mother, food was a precious commodity, and she loved to cook. She felt happy that she could make large, wholesome, delicious meals for the people she loved. In Nicki's house you had to have seconds, and you weren't allowed to waste food by leaving it on your plate. She soon got used to cramming in a few more mouthfuls, even when she felt full to bursting. As she got older, Nicki became aware that she was bigger than the rest of her friends and gradually gave up playing sports, which she loved, because she felt it drew attention to her size. She regarded a thin shape as the only kind that was attractive – and her friends shared these values, even if they weren't nasty to her about her shape. Although she was naturally sporty, by the time she hit her teens Nicki was very overweight. She couldn't find any clothes to fit her in the high street shops and felt too self-conscious to go out to parties and discos with her friends. At 16, she started a series of strict 'diets' such as living on cabbage soup, replacing meals with drinks, or cutting out all carbohydrates. After two weeks of feeling miserable and deprived, she'd go back to the meals she loved so much – often eating more to make up for what she'd missed. She became a typical yo-yo dieter, alternately trying to 'be good' by eating as little as possible and then over-eating and berating herself for being 'greedy'. At 33, she's a busy working mother with a husband and two children who love her, and lots of friends. She has an active lifestyle, so she's slimmer than she's ever been, but she never has a day when she doesn't feel fat and ugly, regardless of her actual weight.

You weren't given enough attention

You may look back and think, 'My childhood was fine,' or 'My parents weren't bad people.' But you don't have to have suffered cruelty or deprivation to have missed out on all the supportive daily actions, signs and messages that tell children they are acceptable, lovable, and good.

ANNA

Anna was a middle child in a family of six children. Her parents were both respected academics and they lived in a large house filled with piles of books and papers, plants and pictures. The children had a lot of freedom – there were no rules about bedtime, or what they wore to school, and they had a huge garden to run around in. Both parents were very busy with their work, and taught the children to be self-sufficient from an early age – making their own lunch-boxes, getting their tea when they came home, and putting themselves to bed at night. But the children got little individual attention – Anna couldn't remember her parents ever coming to one of her school performances or sports days, and she never had a party or special treat for her birthday. At weekends, Anna would often take herself on solitary walks for hours and no one in the house seemed to notice. Her father was susceptible to stress, and when he was under pressure he would frequently explode, accusing the children of making too much noise or moving an important paper. Anna left home at 18 and moved to a big city, where she got a job working in local government, but she finds herself attracted to volatile men who can't commit to her, and has had a series of relationships that have caused her a lot of pain.

You lacked affection

Parents who have not learned from their own parents how to give love freely, or who are stressed, unhappy or preoccupied, may be unable to show the love and affection that their child needs. You may have received some, but not enough, praise, interest, encouragement, warmth and affection.

PAUL

Paul was born three months prematurely and spent weeks in an incubator. He caught a lung infection and for a couple of weeks the doctors warned his parents to expect the worst. He overcame the illness, got stronger and was finally well enough to come home. But he still seemed fragile and tiny to his young mother, who was terrified he'd get ill again. She started getting up several times a night to check that he was still breathing, and became exhausted. Paul was a fretful baby who didn't feed easily and his frequent crying was difficult for his mother. She soon developed post-natal depression, and would leave him in his cot or playpen for hours. Paul's father worked long hours to provide for the family, and got into the habit of going straight to the pub after work to wind down and avoid the tension at home. Paul's grandmother tried to help, by visiting as often as she could and making a big fuss of Paul, so that Paul felt closer to her than to his mother as a child. But shortly after his tenth birthday, his grandmother died. His parents divorced soon after, and his mother remarried and had two more children. Seeing how warm and affectionate she was with them was a stark contrast to his own childhood. Paul did well at school and he left home at 18 to go to university, and later became an engineer. At 40, he often feels lonely – although he joins in with social events at work, he tends to hold people at arm's length and doesn't let anyone get too close.

Your parents had low self-confidence

Your beliefs about yourself and your place in society can be a reflection of how your parents feel about themselves. Unwittingly, they may have passed on their self-doubts or negative beliefs. It can be as simple as your mother saying, 'How could I be so stupid?' to herself every time something went wrong. Or maybe your parents didn't dare question the decision of those in authority, such as doctors or teachers, even when they had doubts about them – you'd hear 'The doctor knows best,' or 'Your teacher knows best.'

MEENA

Meena's father and mother emigrated to England from India and started a dry-cleaning business. Through hard work and good customer service, the business flourished, and soon they had a chain of dry-cleaning shops that provided a comfortable home and lifestyle for them and their two daughters. But they never lost their conviction that, deep down, they weren't 'as good as' the people they mixed with. So although Meena and her younger sister enjoyed a privileged lifestyle of private schools, ballet and horseriding lessons, they also absorbed their parents' messages that they were somehow inferior to the people in their social circle, and that other people's opinions and feelings were more valid than their own. That was the message Meena got from some of her schoolmates too. They overrode her in conversation, made fun of her accent, and giggled behind their hands when she spoke up in class. Meena felt she just didn't fit, and had nothing worthwhile to contribute. When she got a job in public relations, she never complained when more and more work was passed her way – she simply got on with it. Increasingly, she has noticed that her best ideas are hijacked by more confident colleagues in meetings and presented as their own. She has simply shrugged her shoulders and never complained – after all, people will probably not pay much attention if she speaks up. She has never objected when her bosses present her with last-minute work, even though it means working late and coming in at the weekends. But she often feels stressed and wound up, and frustrated that, despite her hard work, her career seems to be going nowhere.

There was no praise

If you were treated as if nothing you did was good enough, and those closest to you focused on your mistakes and weaknesses and ignored your successes and strengths, you may have grown up with the sense that there was something fundamentally wrong with you, or that you were lacking in some way.

JACKSON

Jackson was a lively and boisterous only child whose parents were quiet and reserved. They both believed the worst thing you could do to a child was 'spoil' it, so they were careful never to praise Jackson, in case he got 'big-headed'. His parents were actually very proud of him and between themselves they would talk about how good he was and how well he was doing, but they never said that to him. They would hold back when he came home with a glowing school report, discussing only the few things that needed improvement. Jackson learned that the worst crime in his parents' book was being 'full of yourself'. As he grew up, he tried harder and harder to please his parents and get the praise and approval he so craved, but no matter how hard he tried, nothing ever seemed good enough.

By the time he left home, his parents' standards had become his own. He had become a driven perfectionist. He has quickly climbed the career ladder, but is tormented by the sense that nothing he does quite measures up. He finds it almost impossible to relax and has a nagging sense of guilt whenever he is enjoying himself.

Shock or big changes as an adult

So far, we've concentrated on childhood experiences in this chapter, but in some cases poor self-confidence doesn't develop until adulthood. Experiencing traumatic events as an adult can undermine even healthy self-confidence. Being intimidated or bullied at work, undergoing long-term stress or financial hardship, being in an abusive relationship, being a victim of crime or being involved in an accident – experiences like these can knock your confidence and your sense of your own worth.

CAROL

Carol was a kind and considerate person who was great at putting people at their ease. Although not particularly ambitious, she had worked her way up to become a staff supervisor at a large supermarket, because she was a good manager who always put 100 per cent into her work. Although she had lots of friends, she'd never married or had children. She joked that the people at work were like her 'family' and couldn't manage without her. Her boss used to tell her she kept the place going, and feeling that she was a valued part of an organisation was very important to her. But the year before her 50th birthday her boss retired, and was replaced by a younger man, Jason, who seemed to take an instant dislike to Carol. He didn't like her management style, which he said was too 'informal', and implied that she was too lenient on staff, and spent too much time listening to their problems. He refused to give Carol credit for the fact that the supermarket had the lowest turnover of staff in the whole region. He started overruling her decisions, often in front of other staff members. He also constantly picked fault with Carol's paperwork. She began to suffer from stress, and started to spend time checking and rechecking her work so that she fell behind with deadlines and lost all of her former efficiency. After nine months she resigned, but by that time she had lost all confidence in her abilities. Without her job, she felt she didn't know who she was any more. She knew she should be looking for a new job, but spent her days watching TV at home, rarely leaving the house.

Abuse and neglect

While most of the experiences in this section are common, unfortunately some people have it even worse. If children are treated badly, they often grow up thinking that they 'deserved' it, because they are 'bad'. It's virtually impossible to grow up with healthy self-esteem if you are always on the receiving end of physical or psychological punishments, especially if you have no real idea of why you are being punished. Being sexually abused, neglected or abandoned has a devastating effect on self-image and self-confidence. Not surprisingly, these experiences leave a psychological scar. They affect how you see yourself, and perhaps also your ability to trust other people. By reading this book you've taken a brave step in overcoming your past. People *can* heal a negative self-image caused by abuse or neglect, and find the happiness, peace and stability they deserve. Many people have managed to do this. But delving into such a past can initially bring up pain that may disrupt your life, so you feel worse before you feel better. Working with a professional counsellor or psychotherapist will help guide you through this process in the safest and most effective way. See your GP for a referral or, if you can afford private treatment, contact a therapist through one of the organisations listed on pages 242–3. If you like the approach described in this book, then your best bet might be to look for a skilled cognitive behaviour therapist, experienced in helping people who have been through the same things as you.

THE POWER OF THE PAST OVER THE PRESENT

Have you ever had an experience where, out of nowhere, your emotions and body sensations immediately transported you back to your childhood? Long-forgotten memories can be triggered in startling detail. Facing a tricky meeting at work can bring back the stomach-churning anxiety you felt before every maths lesson at age 10. Finding that a group of work colleagues had a night out without asking you can take you right back to age 13, and the hurt you felt at being left out of a friend's birthday party.

You may have asked yourself how you can still be affected by such seemingly inconsequential things that happened so long ago. After all, since then you've done so much that has proved you are a worthwhile person. Chances are, you have a lot to be pleased about and proud of in your life. So how come your past still has such a strong influence on how you feel – and how you live your life – today?

It comes down to your Bottom Line. Your experiences may have been in the past, but the image that you formed about yourself at the time is still alive and well. It's this Bottom Line – a statement that sums up your view of yourself – that is the basis of your poor self-confidence.

By the time you've worked through this book, you'll have identified your Bottom Line (or Bottom Lines – some people have more than one). To give you an idea, here are the Bottom Lines of the people whose stories you've just read.

Charlotte: *I am a joke*

Kevin: *I am stupid*

Nicki: *I am fat and ugly*

Anna: *I am unimportant*

Paul: *I am unlovable*

Meena: *I am inferior*

Jackson: *I am not good enough*

Carol: *I am incompetent*

Having read their stories, it's easy to see how these people would come to these conclusions about themselves, given their experiences. But you can no doubt see that, just because these conclusions are understandable, it doesn't follow that they are *right*. Did *you* think Jackson wasn't good enough, Paul was unlovable and Anna was unimportant? Did *you* come to the conclusion that Carol was incompetent, Charlotte a joke, Nicki fat and ugly, and Meena inferior?

As an unbiased observer, what would you say to these people if you met them tomorrow? Would you tell Charlotte that she has a rare and special gift, and that it was her parents' narrow values that prevented them from appreciating and nurturing that talent? Would you point out that Kevin's slowness to learn was nothing to do with stupidity, but more a consequence of lack of awareness of dyslexia at the time? Would you tell Carol that she feels incompetent not because she is, but because she's been the victim of a systematic bullying campaign? Would you want Paul to know that his mother's inability to bond with him was a tragic consequence of the depression she suffered, and not any fault of his own? Would you reassure Jackson that his parents did not praise him because they thought it would make him swollen-headed, not because he wasn't good enough? Would you tell Anna that it was her parents' all-engrossing careers that made them pay her so little attention, not Anna herself? Would you tell Nicki that she isn't fat and ugly and that her weight is only one aspect of who she is, and not a very important one at that? Would you tell Meena that the messages her parents gave her came from their own feelings of low self-confidence, not because she is worth less than other people?

Apart from Carol, these people all formed their Bottom Lines in childhood. So it would not be surprising if their views were inaccurate, given that they were originally a child's eye view. In all probability, when your Bottom Line was formed, you were too young to understand what was really going on and to question whether it was valid to conclude that you were unlovable, stupid, or whatever. You would not have been able to see how your reaction was based on a misunderstanding. After all, it didn't occur to your three-year-old self to question the idea of one man delivering presents to all the children in the world on the same night!

TIME TO GET WRITING:

Pinning down your Bottom Line

Now, think about your own view of yourself and the experiences that fed into it, while you were growing up and perhaps also later in your life. Are you getting an idea of what your Bottom Line might be? Don't worry if it's still not clear at this stage, or you have several Bottom Lines, or you're not entirely happy with the wording – as you progress through the book it will become clearer. And understanding where your Bottom Line came from is the first step to creating natural self-confidence.

How to do it:

Take a pen and paper and, in as much detail as you can, jot down the thoughts that spring to mind as you read through the following questions:

What do you say about yourself when you are being self-critical?

What names do you call yourself when you are angry and frustrated?

What were the words people in your life used to describe you when they were angry or disappointed in you?

What messages about yourself did you pick up from your parents, other members of your family or your peers?

If you can, cast your mind back to the time when you first starting feeling as you do now about yourself. Was there a single event which crystallised your ideas about yourself? Or was there a sequence of events over time? Or perhaps a general atmosphere, such as one of disapproval, rather than specific events?

If you could capture the essence of your doubts about yourself in a single sentence ('I am . . .') what would it be? Write it here:

Now take time to reflect on what you've written and ask yourself the simple question, Is this *really* true? If a friend had gone through the same kind of experiences as you, would you judge them as negatively as you judge yourself? Chances are you'd find it easy to separate the circumstances from who they are as a person, and you'd be able to truthfully tell them that it simply wasn't their fault that someone in their life behaved badly, judged them, had unrealistic expectations of them or whatever. Now it's time to apply this compassion and this kind of thinking – emotionally intelligent thinking – to *yourself*. You need to see that your Bottom Line, your inaccurate self-image, isn't actually who you are – it's just a rather skewed *opinion* of who you are.

You now have a choice. You can back away from the challenge in this book and carry on believing your Bottom Line to be true. After all, accepting that your basic self-image is wrong can be quite a frightening prospect. Sometimes sticking with what you know can feel safer, even if it makes you unhappy.

Or, could you take a leap and open your mind to the possibility that your self-image is unfair and inaccurate?

You know that there is a part of you that wants change, or you wouldn't be reading this book. So can you accept the idea that you may have reached conclusions about yourself based on misunderstandings, or blamed yourself for something that was not your fault?

WHY IS IT HARD TO QUESTION THE WAY YOU THINK?

Don't worry if it's a difficult prospect to view your experiences objectively. Your Bottom Line exerts its influence over you in many ways, one of which is changing the way you think. Powerful beliefs produce a kind of 'thinking filter' that makes your mind home in on experiences that are consistent with your beliefs, and screen out experiences that contradict them. Here are two thinking filters that contribute to your lack of self-confidence and keep the Bottom Line going:

1 Only seeing the bad

Pregnant women and their partners often say that it seems as if half the world is pregnant – they seem to see pregnant women or newborn babies everywhere. The truth is that their minds are simply homing in on pregnancy – before they got pregnant, they probably didn't even register many of the pregnant women walking past them in the street. Another example is that if you're considering buying a certain model of car, you suddenly see them all over the place.

A similar thing happens when your self-confidence is low – your mind's radar system is tuned in to pick up on anything that confirms the negative ideas you have about yourself (your Bottom Line). So when you look at yourself in the mirror in the morning, your focus zooms, like a heat-seeking missile, to your frizzy hair, dimply thighs, pimply skin or whatever it is about your appearance that you feel lets you down. As the day goes on, your mind keeps you updated with personalised 'news flashes' of exactly how you've messed up, or fallen short, *once again*. 'You sounded like a mumbling idiot in that meeting.' 'How could you have forgotten to renew the car tax?' 'You're so dull – why can't you be more outgoing and relaxed at parties?' 'Another evening slumped in front of the TV – you're so lazy.'

At the same time, all the things that actually *disprove* your Bottom Line (your freshly washed hair, your natural smile, your patience and tolerance, your self-motivation, and so on) fall so far below your radar that most of the time you don't even register them. The end result is that as you go through life you generally focus on what you're doing wrong, not on what you're doing right.

Are you beginning to see why it's difficult for you to get an accurate view of your true strengths and good qualities?

2 Putting a negative spin on everything

Sometimes stuff just happens, but to the self-critical mind nothing is random – it's all your fault at some level, or it's happened because you're a failure in some way. Lacking self-confidence means that your thinking is consistently biased in favour of self-criticism. But this not only affects what your mind homes in on, it also affects how you *interpret* what happens. So not only do slip-ups, mishaps and mistakes loom large in your mind, they also become the basis for making judgements about yourself.

Suppose a friend texts to say they can't meet you after all. You discount the reason they offer and substitute your own interpretation – you're too boring to spend time with, or they don't want to be your friend any more. Or one day you get called into school because your child is falling behind in class. The teacher suggests a number of reasons why this may be happening, but in your mind there's only one reason – your failure as a parent. Another time, you didn't get an interview for a job that more than 200 people applied for. It must mean that you're a loser that no one in their right mind would want to employ.

A mind that lacks self-confidence can even put its own special 'spin' on *positive* experiences. Someone admires your new outfit? – 'They're just being polite.' Your boss compliments your efficiency? – 'I've managed to fool him again.'

HOW FILTERED THINKING FEEDS YOUR LOW SELF-CONFIDENCE

These thinking filters mean that while it's easy to see other people's situations objectively (for example, that Kevin isn't stupid, or that Charlotte isn't a joke), it's very hard to take a step back and look objectively at your own beliefs. You focus on the downside of future, present and past events. As a result, the memories you store all tend to have a negative slant. So, when you're faced with a new situation and your mind is trawling through its memory bank for similar experiences, it will come up with only negative memories. Not surprisingly, that means you're already anticipating – and on the alert for – things that could go wrong. If you're feeling low and bad about yourself, your mind is ready to run its specially edited, personal DVD entitled 'Reasons you should be feeling bad/Things you've messed up in the past/ Times you've felt embarrassed, hurt or rejected'. Your filters not only keep your Bottom Line in place, but they also do a very efficient job of making you feel anxious and unhappy.

Why is negative thinking so powerful?

There is a theory that the reason the brain finds it so easy to focus on the negative is that it's a hang-over from our days as hunter-gatherers when danger (being attacked by an animal or another human) lurked everywhere. Our lifestyles have changed, but this built-in, automatic 'fight or flight' survival mechanism is still in place. And, because as human beings we have language and imagination, it's thoughts and images in the mind's eye that set off our alarm signals – we don't need a real tiger, we can create one in our heads.

➢ *FIND OUT MORE ABOUT THIS:* Turn to chapter 4 to find out more about how anxious thinking feeds low self-confidence. Chapters 5 and 8 have more about self-criticism and how you can change your Bottom Line.

INTRODUCING YOUR RULES FOR LIVING

The idea of 'Rules for Living' was introduced at the start of this chapter. Now it's time to look at the role these rules play in undermining your self-confidence.

Your Rules for Living are like your personal instruction manual for life. They're the principles you live by (consciously or unconsciously) on a day-to-day basis. Their primary purpose is to help you make your way in the world, and be accepted by those around you, given that your Bottom Line tells you that you're inadequate, unattractive, unlovable, or whatever it is. Developing Rules for Living is a natural survival instinct – this is how you've learned to avoid criticism or rejection or being judged by other people. They're a kind of shield that helps you feel OK about yourself. But although your Rules are initially useful, as time goes on they simply keep your Bottom Line in place and keep your self-confidence suppressed. Perhaps the easiest way to explain Rules for Living is to look at some examples – take a look at the chart on p. 42, which shows the people we met earlier in the chapter.

How the Rules work

The Rules for Living each of these people developed genuinely help them to get by, given that they assume their Bottom Lines are true. For example, Paul keeps people at arm's length and rarely opens up. He'd love a long-term relationship and feels lonely much of the time but not letting people get close means he's not at risk of rejection. If people don't know me very well, he reasons, they won't see how unlovable I really am.

In many cases, these strategies have positive pay-offs – otherwise they wouldn't persist. Meena's low expectations of how she deserves to be treated meant that when she first landed a good entry-level position in PR, her uncomplaining, 'just-get-on-with-it' attitude went down well and initially earned her respect. Here was someone who could be relied on. But eventually, her Rules for Living began to work against her. She never questions why the mundane, administrative work is always passed to her, and she does it very well. As a result, her boss assumes she is more comfortable with unchallenging work. She lets others take credit for her creative ideas, so she's never viewed as an innovative thinker. Younger colleagues are climbing the career ladder above her and taking on interesting projects she would love to get her teeth into. All this confirms what she

	Bottom Line	Rules for Living
Charlotte	I am a joke	What I do is only worthwhile if other people recognise it as such
Kevin	I am stupid	Unless you're sure you will succeed, don't even try
Nicki	I am fat and ugly	I can only feel good about myself if I've controlled what I've eaten each day and I like what the scales say
Anna	I am unimportant	I must be self-sufficient and expect no help from anyone
Paul	I am unlovable	If I try to get to close to anyone, they will see how unlovable I am and reject me
		If I ask for what I need, I will be disappointed
Meena	I am inferior	So long as I keep my head down and get on with it, I'll be accepted
	I am a misfit	If I say what I think, people will ridicule or dismiss me
Jackson	I am not good enough	I must do everything 110% or I will never get anywhere in life
		If someone criticises me, it means I have failed to measure up
Carol	I am incompetent	If someone puts me down, they must have good reason

secretly believes – she's inferior, with nothing worthwhile to contribute. She often leaves work feeling frustrated and churned up.

➤ *FIND OUT MORE ABOUT THIS:* We'll explore Rules for Living in more detail in Chapter 7, when you'll find out how your own Rules affect the way you think, feel and act. You'll also start work on ditching your Rules and experiment on how to live without them.

ESSENTIAL TAKE-HOME MESSAGES FROM THIS CHAPTER

- Your negative beliefs about yourself (your Bottom Line) may feel like the truth, but in fact they are your opinions, not reality.
- You formed these beliefs as a result of your experiences, usually in early life. Given your experiences, what you believe makes perfect sense. But that doesn't make it true.
- The way you think keeps your Bottom Line in place. Lack of confidence creates 'thinking filters' that stop you from seeing things clearly. These filters seem to produce evidence proving your Bottom Line is true.
- You made up your Rules for Living to help you feel better about yourself, and fit in with the world around you. They are designed to help you get by and, in fact, they probably do have pay-offs. But, in the long run, they keep your Bottom Line in place and suppress your self-confidence.

Life Lesson

Looking for the causes of your low self-confidence is not about apportioning blame or wallowing in self-pity. It's simply the first part of a fact-finding mission that will help you to feel content with yourself and able to live your life to the full.

3

GETTING TO KNOW YOU – WHAT STOPS YOUR SELF-CONFIDENCE GROWING

So far, you have learned how the roots of your lack of self-confidence can be found in your individual life experiences.

In this chapter, you will . . .

- Learn what is stopping your self-confidence from flourishing, even though, chances are, you've also had some positive life experiences.
- Look at what happens when you're put in situations where you fear you might have to break your Rules for Living – for example, where you feel you'll fall short of those self-imposed standards of perfection, or you won't be able to stop an emotional outburst, or control what you eat.

You're no longer that shy kid who didn't quite fit in at school, or you've done well at work despite your parents telling you that you'd never get anywhere in life. Or you have a partner who thinks the world of you, even though you grew up thinking you weren't acceptable. Your life may have changed, but the way you feel about yourself inside hasn't. It's time to look at how the way you think and act on a daily basis keeps your lack of self-confidence going, holding you back from fulfilling your full potential, or experiencing true contentment.

The last chapter explained the idea of your own personal set of Rules for Living. The anxious feelings and self-critical thoughts triggered the threat of breaking these rules are like oxygen to your Bottom Line, fanning the embers so that your negative beliefs flare up again. Being caught in this perpetual cycle is what stops you from moving on, seeing your Bottom Line objectively, renewing your self-image and letting your self-confidence flourish.

By the end of the chapter, you should be able to simplify this experience into a personal flowchart, like the one shown on page 50. The first step is a fact-finding mission. No one enjoys feeling anxious, so ignoring, suppressing or distracting yourself from these feelings is understandable, but it's time to do the opposite and to *sit with* your feelings. This means allowing yourself to experience your feelings as fully as you can without getting tangled up in them or identifying with them. The aim of your fact-finding mission is to identify what happens when your Bottom Line is activated. What fears (anxious predictions) come to mind? What happens then to your emotions, and what physical changes take place in your body? What actions do you take as a result, and afterwards what thoughts go through you head, and how do you feel about yourself?

Think of this as detective work, or being your own therapist, or simply getting to know the most important person in your life – you. Your feelings, thoughts and memories are your biggest clues here.

BREAKING THE RULES

Your Rules for Living affect your emotions in two ways. Firstly, they create threats. The threat of fearing you may be about to break your Rules creates feelings of anxiety. For example, you may feel threatened by the thought that you might not make a deadline at work, or that a new person you just met didn't seem to warm to you. Secondly, once you know for sure (you have confirmation) that your Rules *have* been broken (you missed the deadline, you found out the person you met didn't think much of you), it's likely you'll experience a different kind of emotion, such as sadness and feeling low. Both threats and confirmations can be either big events or small everyday happenings. Either way, the end result is that your Bottom Line feels more real than ever, and your self-confidence takes another knock.

As we discussed earlier, at first your Rules for Living can seem like your best friend. But it's a toxic friendship that in the long run does you more harm than good. Unhelpful and unrealistic Rules make you jump through hoops by placing demands on you that are impossible to meet, such as being perfect at everything you do, being liked by everyone you meet, always having control over your emotions, or never revealing the real you. Letting your Rules control your life means you're living on a knife-edge. You can't win with these Rules – it's simply impossible – so your natural self-confidence takes knock after knock, and your Bottom Line remains alive and kicking.

Living by the Rules is why certain situations seem to have profound effects on you while they barely register with other people. Having a neighbour call in to see you before you've had a chance to clear the breakfast dishes away may upset you for the rest of the day, if your Rules for Living include being always considered organised and in control. Or you may fret for weeks over having to ask a friend to return a book they borrowed from you (which they've simply forgotten about) if your Rules include having to be liked and approved of by everyone. Your reaction to what could be viewed as a totally innocuous situation may seem silly, over-the-top or irritating to people who don't hold the same Bottom Line.

In some cases, the events which have triggered your Bottom Line seem so inconsequential you hardly notice them. You're left with your feelings churned up, or a mild sense of anxiety, and no real idea what's caused it. You may simply tell yourself to 'pull yourself together', seek reassurance from a good friend or partner, or try to suppress the feelings with comfort food or a bottle of wine or your favourite trash TV show. It's time to tune your awareness into patterns like this to unearth what triggers them in the first place.

Avoiding thoughts about anxiety-inducing events and feelings is an understandable protective mechanism. But it's only by doing the opposite, and putting a big mental asterisk on the everyday situations you find challenging or threatening, that you'll begin to understand why your Bottom Line is still going strong. By becoming sensitive to your changes in mood, you'll develop a kind of early-warning system that alerts you to situations that are fuelling your Bottom Line and crushing your self-confidence. By observing the thoughts, feelings and behaviour that follow these situations, you can spot the cycle that keeps your Bottom Line activated – and stop it in its tracks.

Take a few moments to reflect on the week that's just passed. Can you pinpoint any moments when you felt anxious, ill at ease or uncomfortable with yourself? Scan your memory for moments of doubt or panic at your ability to cope or to do something well. Look for times when you seemed plagued by niggling worries about what other people were thinking about you, or when your critical inner voice seemed louder than normal. Jot down as much detail as you can – where, when, why and how the situation occurred.

Now, can you spot any patterns emerging that might hold clues to your Rules for Living? Could that mix of guilt and anxiety you felt at not meeting a (probably unrealistic) work deadline suggest that one of your Rules for Living is that you must do the right thing at all times to be seen as 'good enough'? That not making a deadline must be your fault rather than someone else's bad organisation or unrealistic expectations? Did your sense of panic at discovering that one of the two friends you were meeting for lunch has cancelled suggest that you feel you're not interesting enough to be the subject of one person's sole attention for a whole hour? Writing down the ideas about yourself that came into your head at those moments can give you valuable insight into your Bottom Line.

WHAT KEEPS YOU LACKING IN LOW SELF-CONFIDENCE?

Once your Bottom Line is active, it sets off a vicious circle fuelled by anxious predictions and self-critical thinking, which keeps it firmly in place and may even make it stronger. The following flowchart shows you how this works. Later in the chapter, you'll have a chance to map out your own personal vicious circle, so as you read on, think about how it may apply to you.

The vicious circle that keeps you stuck with
low self-confidence

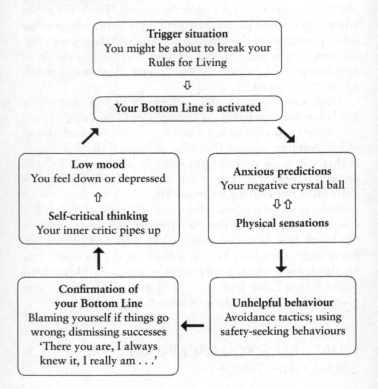

Anxious predictions: Your negative crystal ball

Once a situation has activated your Bottom Line, fears and
anxieties about what will happen next are never far behind.
This is your brain in self-protection mode – it's feeling
threatened, so it's trying to predict exactly where the threat

will come from. It's as if your mind is a crystal ball that can only predict bad things happening in the future.

It may seem counter-intuitive, but to help you understand just how powerful anxious predictions can be, what you're going to do now is to deliberately generate some anxious predictions, so you can get an idea of the kind of fears your mind produces – and how your body reacts to them. But rather than actually putting yourself into a threatening situation, you're going to use the power of imagination, because your body and emotions tend to react in a similar way to real and imagined events. Close your eyes, and imagine yourself standing up in front of an audience of thirty people and giving a twenty-minute talk. Fill in as much detail as possible – visualise what you'd wear, the size of the room, the temperature, how you'd walk into the room, whether you'd be holding notes or using PowerPoint, where you'd stand, how many people would be there, what they'd be sitting on, etc. Now, let your imagination take over and fill in what happens next.

When people who lack self-confidence do this exercise, they usually imagine the worst and see it all going terribly wrong. Did you picture yourself going bright red in the face and everyone staring? Did you see yourself completely clamming up or stammering over your words? Perhaps you saw the audience looking bored and slightly irritated by having to listen to you? Or looking at you with pity because you're clearly not up to the job and are embarrassing yourself? Or did people start to question you and challenge the accuracy of what you were saying, or simply start shouting 'That's rubbish!'?

These are what are known as 'anxious predictions' and they come from your Bottom Line. Just as the situations that activate the Bottom Line vary from person to person, so the exact nature of the anxious predictions will vary from person to person too, depending on what is most important to them. Anxious predictions can have a powerful impact on your feelings and on your behaviour.

Physical sensations

You probably noticed that simply visualising this situation produced physical changes. Your heartbeat may have quickened and your breathing become quicker and more shallow. Maybe you could feel the muscles in the back of your neck and shoulders tightening, or your stomach started to churn. These are all signs of anxiety, the body's instinctive response to threat – real or imagined. Not surprisingly, once these physical sensations have kicked in, they compound your anxiety by triggering more anxious predictions. If your mouth goes dry, you could worry that you won't be able to speak. If your heart is beating fast, it's not easy to think clearly, and it could convince you that your mind's about to go blank.

➤ *FIND OUT MORE ABOUT THIS:* Turn to Chapter 4 to learn how to tune into your own personal warning signs that you're looking into that negative crystal ball – and how to question and test your anxious predictions.

Given that anxious predictions can produce such an uncomfortable reaction, you probably won't be surprised to learn that people do what they can to avoid situations which trigger them. Here are some of the ways you may do it.

Avoidance tactics

Ever pretended you were ill so you could cancel a date at the last minute because you were so nervous about going? Or told someone you were busy so you didn't have to go to an intimidating party? Or turned your phone off rather than deal with a tricky phone call? They're all different versions of the same thing – avoidance tactics. In the short term, they feel great – you get an immediate sense of relief that you've side-stepped a threatening or unpleasant situation. But the truth is that what you have done unknowingly guarantees that you will feel just as anxious the next time you face something similar.

By avoiding the situation, you have denied yourself a chance to find out what really would have happened. It could be that actually things would have gone much better than you predicted – you might have had a perfectly pleasant date, or enjoyed the party. The phone call might not have been half as tricky as you expected. But because you've avoided the situation, you'll never find out, so you have no evidence to contradict your anxious predictions, ensuring they will continue to run riot in your mind whenever you're faced with a similar situation. So although avoidance tactics may help you feel better in the short term, in the long term it's like living your life in an invisible cage.

Later on in this book you'll look at how you might start facing your threatening situations rather than avoiding them. You may feel sick to the stomach even at the thought of this and wonder how on earth it could help. Facing your fears is about two things: first you get hold of accurate, up-to-date information, and then you experiment with acting differently and discovering what happens. As you extend your range, self-confidence grows. Getting information and experimenting are crucial parts of the jigsaw you are piecing together – building a new and more compassionate self-image.

Taking too many precautions: 'safety-seeking'

An alternative to simply avoiding situations that trigger anxiety is to go into the situation, but only after you've put a number of what we call 'precautions' in place, designed to stop your predictions from coming true. Psychologists call these precautions 'safety-seeking behaviours' and you can see why – you want to stop the worst happening and stay safe. At the time they may do just that, and let you feel you've narrowly escaped disaster, but the irony is that in the long term they stop you from updating your perspective, and keep you stuck in low self-confidence. They may even make things worse. For example, if your safety-seeking behaviour was taking care to reveal very little about yourself out of fear that people won't like the 'real you', you could come across as aloof and stand-offish and find it difficult to make friends.

Let's think how our friends from Chapter 2 might seek safety before going in front of an audience. Jackson, whose Rules for Living include always doing something 110 per cent, would spend hours researching his speech, then rehearse it over and over until he felt it was a 110 per cent performance. He would also make sure his talk filled all the time, so there'd be no time for questions he might not be able to answer, and he wouldn't contemplate deviating from the script. He'd appear confident and competent but would avoid making any eye contact or engaging with the audience in case something unexpected came up that he was not fully prepared to deal with.

Charlotte, by contrast, would spend hours trying to second-guess what her audience would like to hear, and ask as many friends and colleagues as she could for their opinions on what she should say, to make up for her own shortcomings. She might find out what approach was taken by the last person who gave a similar presentation, and tailor her speech to match. During the presentation, she'd be scanning the room for signs that people were taking her seriously.

So long as your self-protection measures are in place, you will always credit them with saving you from disaster. Just like avoidance tactics, self-protective measures don't allow you to find out for yourself whether or not your anxious predictions were accurate. If things go OK, you will be left with the sense that your success was entirely due to the precautions you took. Your feelings of self-worth and self-confidence depend on that success, so you are locking yourself into this pattern of behaviour in the future.

It's only by approaching a threatening situation without your usual precautions in place that you will grow more confident and content with yourself. You need to discover for yourself that you can get by without them.

CONFIRMATION OF YOUR BOTTOM LINE

What if you go ahead and things go wrong?

Let's face it, even confident people get a little nervous at times, especially if they're doing something like public speaking. But they realise that a few tummy flutters or sweaty palms are perfectly normal and not major hurdles to overcome.

It's a very different story if you lack self-confidence. If you can't stand back and observe your anxiety as normal, and instead interpret it as a sign that something is about to go wrong, there is a chance that you've created a self-fulfilling prophecy – by over-reacting to normal nervousness, you ensure that things don't go well. Your mind goes blank, or you can't stop yourself blushing, sweating or shaking. And of course, instead of being able to see that anxiety got the better of you, you put the situation down to your incompetence, stupidity and general uselessness. What has happened seems to confirm your Bottom Line and, once more, your self-confidence takes a knock. You may feel like crawling into a small hole and staying there.

It may be hard to imagine right now, but when you get to the end of the book you should be in a place where you can see your weakness and slip-ups as just a small part of what makes you an individual, and not evidence that confirms your lack of worth as a person.

And what if it goes well?

If you have healthy self-confidence, and you do something that's a bit out of your comfort zone and find that, on the whole, it went pretty well, you'll justifiably walk with a spring in your step the next day, or at least give yourself a mental pat on the back for your achievement. You'd probably also do a mental update of your view of your skills and ability in that area. But it's a different story for someone whose self-confidence has been damaged. Maybe you'd feel a temporary lift in mood because of the relief that it's all over, but your success is unlikely to make a long-term difference to the way you see yourself. Why? Because a person with low self-esteem would put the success down to chance or good luck rather than anything they did. Or they'd dismiss the achievement altogether ('If I managed to do it, then it couldn't have been that hard'). Or they'll focus on the one tiny part that didn't go quite so well.

If your underlying view of yourself is strongly negative, you'll feel compelled to discount anything that doesn't fit in with this view. It's a bit like being prejudiced against yourself – your mind screens out evidence that contradicts your Bottom Line. You dismiss positive achievements: unlike the things that go wrong, your achievements don't count. Let's take Jackson as an example. His boss returns ten pieces of work to him. Nine have no corrections, but the tenth has a few red pen marks indicating changes he wants made. All Jackson focuses on is the red pen marks. He feels a failure for the rest of the week – the fact that these were minor changes, and the other reports didn't need any at all, is irrelevant to him. Once again, he has failed to measure up.

➤ *FIND OUT MORE ABOUT THIS:* Turn to Chapter 6 to learn how to notice and take pleasure in your achievements and in the good things in your life.

CONFIDENCE AND SELF-CRITICAL THINKING

When you've had an experience that confirms your Bottom Line, self-critical thoughts are never far behind. As soon as your Rules of Living have been threatened or broken, your critical self-commentary kicks in to let you know that you were absolutely right – you *are* useless, stupid, boring, unlovable, or whatever really. Sometimes, you may actually say this aloud: 'There you go, just as I always knew, I shouldn't even try to do anything like this because I'm always useless at it.' Or it may be more intangible than that – a feeling, without words, that you carry round. For some, it's a hollowness in the chest, or it could be a sinking feeling in the stomach, or a sense that your nerves are on edge. You may feel vulnerable, insecure or just low. Or you might go into fantasy mode, and lose yourself in unrealistic mental images of the kind of perfect, flawless, effortlessly capable and popular person you wish you were, and think deep down that you should be.

Self-critical thoughts have a big impact on how you feel

and how you deal with your life, whether they come and go in a split second – 'Why are you such an idiot?' – or develop into detailed tirades – 'You are such a completely useless waste of space. You're pathetic. You're an embarrassment. Everyone was laughing at you today. Why do you even bother trying, when you always mess things up?'. If you've struggled with your weight, you no doubt have a loud inner critic that berates you if you eat even a tiny bit more than you planned – 'You have no willpower, you're such a greedy pig, no wonder you're so fat, you just never know when to stop, people must think you're disgusting . . .' It's not difficult to see how a verbal tirade like that will affect your mood – telling yourself you're an unacceptable failure isn't exactly going to motivate you, make you feel good about yourself, excited by life and the future, and capable of anything.

So far the emphasis has been that your thoughts are not always reliable, but that doesn't mean they're not powerful. Imagine if someone was constantly putting you down, always pointing out your mistakes or things that you're unhappy with; or telling you that you're no good and there's no point in you trying anything; or being angry with you. Naturally, this would increase your stress levels and make you feel anxious and upset, even depressed. Nothing surprising in that. But could this be what you're doing to yourself – that it's your *own* thoughts and imagination hounding you? If you're constantly putting *yourself* down, almost inevitably your mood will plummet and you'll start to feel depressed. And we know from research that low mood itself puts a toxic spin on the way you think. Suddenly, you simply can't bring to mind anything positive about yourself, your past, your present or future. Needless to say, this ensures that your self-confidence remains well and truly crushed.

➢ *FIND OUT MORE ABOUT THIS:* Turn to Chapter 5 to learn about how to detect and answer your self-critical thoughts, and to treat yourself with more compassion.

🖉 *TIME TO GET WRITING:*

Mapping your own vicious circle

By now you should have some personal insights into when you start looking into your negative crystal ball or making anxious predictions, what you do to avoid or minimise the impact of the threatening events that you predict, and the self-critical thoughts that typically run through your mind as a result. Focusing on these thoughts and emotions isn't easy, and you may have felt like giving up to go and do something else. Please stay with it for this final exercise – it's the most crucial part of the chapter – then treat yourself to a well-earned break.

How to do it

You'll need a blank sheet of A4 paper, a pencil and eraser. Use the flowchart on page 50 as your guide as you begin to map your own vicious circle.

Trigger situation. Start by thinking of a situation which you've noticed comes up again and again, and regularly creates feelings of anxiety or uncertainty. This is your 'Trigger situation': write that down as the first heading. Find a recent example, so that you can think in terms of nitty gritty details, rather than vague, general terms that may be less helpful to you. Describe the situation in one or two sentences. Then go round the flowchart filling it in as described below.

Anxious predictions. In that situation, what exactly did you think might happen? Write down everything you thought might go wrong.

Physical sensations. When these predictions were in your mind, how did you feel? Did your heart race, your stomach feel fluttery, your muscles tense up, your body temperature rise? Visualise your threatening situation in as much detail as you can so you can really conjure up the anxious feelings it created. Write them down.

Unhelpful behaviour. What did you do to stop your predictions from coming true? Did you avoid the situation altogether? Did you go into the situation, but take precautions to protect yourself?

Confirmation of your Bottom Line. How did you judge yourself after the situation was over? Did you notice your performance was hampered by anxiety and blame yourself? Or was everything fine, but you dismissed your success? Did you have the sense that what happened just confirmed your unkind opinion of yourself, supporting your Bottom Line? How did you experience this? Did you put it into words ('There you are, I always knew it, I really am . . .'? Or was it more of a feeling?

Self-critical thinking. What exactly did you say to yourself afterwards? What sort of put-downs did you use? What sort of names did you call yourself?

Low mood. Feeling down or even depressed. What was your experience of this? Notice its effect on your body and behaviour (e.g. feeling drained, wanting to hide yourself away).

IT'S TIME TO STEP OUT OF THIS VICIOUS CIRCLE

Look at the map you've created. You can probably see that it illustrates the vicious circle that stops your self-confidence growing and keeps your Bottom Line alive and well. If you follow the exercises throughout the rest of the book, you'll discover ways of breaking the circle and discovering a new, kinder and more accepting way of relating to yourself.

You'll learn how to . . .

- Identify when your mind has gone into 'anxious prediction' mode.
- Take a step back from your fearful thoughts and ask, 'Is this really true?'
- Push the boundaries of your comfort zone so you find out through actual experience just how accurate your anxious predictions are.
- Wise up to self-critical thinking and be aware of its link to depression.
- Take that negative spin off the way you view your personal strengths and individual talents.
- Change your unhelpful Rules for Living.
- Tackle your Bottom Line head on and finally remove the block that stops your natural self-confidence from blossoming.

ESSENTIAL TAKE-HOME MESSAGES FROM THIS CHAPTER

- Every day, your thoughts, feelings and emotions keep your low self-confidence going. They create a vicious circle – you doubt yourself, so you focus on what might go wrong, and anxious predictions follow.

- You do your best to protect yourself and stop your predictions from coming true, by avoiding situations completely, or taking unnecessary precautions. You blame yourself for shortfalls in performance, noticing only the negative aspects and discounting your achievements. The end result is that your deeply held negative beliefs about yourself seem more convincing than ever.
- Breaking the circle is the key to improving your self-confidence. Drawing your own vicious circle is the first step in doing this.

Life Lesson

One of your biggest enemies is self-critical thinking – that negative voice in your head that tells you how useless, stupid or unlovable you are. Because this voice is loud and persistent, it feels true. It can affect your mood so powerfully that in some cases it can trigger full-blown depression.

4

HOW TO STOP ANXIETY HOLDING YOU BACK

You don't have to be an astrologer to make predictions – we all do it, every day of our lives, and we act on these predictions. Most of the time you may not even notice you're doing it or put your predictions into words. You don't have a running commentary that says 'If I press this button, I'll turn on the TV . . .', or 'If I press down on this pedal, the car will slow down,' but nonetheless you're subconsciously making and acting on predictions like these all the time. Other predictions are more thought out and conscious ('If I leave now, I can catch the 5.30'). Predictions are usually based on experience, and we use information from what happens to amend and update predictions if necessary so that they'll stay useful ('I need to leave ten minutes earlier than yesterday, if I'm to catch the 5.30').

Chapter 3 showed how predictions can work against you when you have low self-confidence. When your Bottom Line is negative, it's hard to make accurate predictions. In situations where your self-protective Rules for Living *might*

be broken (you *might* produce a less than perfect performance, someone *might* not approve of you), you become
filled with feelings of self-doubt. This means that instead
of standing back and making realistic predictions based on
past experience, you're more likely to anticipate the worst:
'I'll mess up', 'They'll laugh at me', 'I'm going to look so
stupid', 'I'll lose my job', 'He'll never speak to me again',
'I won't be able to cope.' You have no evidence to back
up anxious predictions, but they feel true. So you think,
'Better safe than sorry,' and take steps to make sure they
won't come true. These are the 'safety-seeking behaviours'
or unnecessary precautions introduced in Chapter 3.

The flowchart on the opposite page is an overview of
how this works. As you can see, you're most likely to
start making anxious predictions when there's an element
of doubt or uncertainty. When you're not entirely sure
what will happen, your mind fills in the gaps with fearful imaginings, often coming up with the very worst that
could happen. There's probably a part of you that knows
the worst is very unlikely, or at least realises that the situation won't actually harm you, and there's a chance you'd
be able to cope. But the more anxious you feel, the more
believable and threatening your predictions become.

Take **Tara** – an attractive woman who is friendly and
chatty at work and in the playground when she drops off
her kids. But her friends have begun to notice that when
they ask her to join them for a drink, or to come for dinner
or to a party, she always has some excuse why she can't
make it. Some assume she's too busy, others decide she
doesn't like them enough to spend an evening with them.
The truth is that Tara's Bottom Line ('I am boring') comes
to life at the thought of socialising in a group. She was
bullied from the ages of 12 to 16 at school. She was teased

Your Rules *might* be broken

↓

Self-doubt and uncertainty:
Your Bottom Line is activated

↓

Anxious predictions

↓

Physical and mental signs of anxiety

↓

Self-protective manoeuvres kick in (avoidance, or
safety-seeking behaviours)

↓

No chance to check out and update anxious predictions

↓

Your Bottom Line remains unchanged

and told by the in-crowd that she was 'too boring' to join
in with them. Tara has tried hard to put her teenage years
behind her but she still believes that she just isn't interesting
or entertaining enough. There is a part of her that knows
she can make people laugh, and that people seem interested
when she talks. But she avoids most group social events,
or goes overboard being the life and soul of the party if
she does go – so she never gets a chance to test out her
anxious prediction that 'People will ignore me or make fun
of me', and find out if it is really true. If she did say yes to
a social event, she could discover for herself that she is no
more boring than anyone else, and that in fact people are

quite happy for her simply to be herself. There is no need for her to make constant efforts to be entertaining. This is how anxious predictions, and the things you do to protect yourself against the worst happening, hold you back, and stop your self-confidence from blossoming.

In this chapter, you will learn how to . . .

- Spot the early-warning signs that you're going into 'anxious prediction' mode.
- Identify your anxious predictions.
- Uncover the unnecessary precautions you take to stop your anxious predictions from coming true.
- Question the validity of your anxious predictions and come up with more helpful alternatives.
- Check out, by experimenting with operating in a different way, how true your anxious predictions really are.
- Replace your anxious predictions with something more useful and realistic.

CHECKING OUT ANXIOUS PREDICTIONS: FIVE VITAL STEPS

Step 1: Tune into your anxiety

Anxiety has a physical effect and produces a range of body sensations that are so common, they've entered everyday language – we talk about 'quivering with fear' or 'going white as a sheet'.

Read through the list of symptoms below, and put a cross by any that feel familiar to you:

- *Muscle tension.* You may start clenching or grinding your jaw, or hunching your shoulders. Your neck or your head may ache or you may start to frown. You may even find you start to shake.

- *Breathing abnormally.* Does your breathing speed up, or become more shallow, or more uneven? Or do you find yourself holding your breath or over-breathing and feeling light-headed, dizzy or faint?

- *Mood changes.* It may be harder to focus and concentrate. You may find your mind goes blank, or you feel confused and muddled by normally simple tasks. In extreme cases, you may find your vision blurs or you start to get tunnel vision.

- *Effect on your stomach or bowels.* Your stomach starts churning, you feel sick or you may feel a desperate need to go to the toilet, even though you only went ten minutes ago!

- *Heart rate changes.* Do you suddenly become aware of your heart beating in your chest, because it seems to be pounding, beating faster or skipping a beat?

- *Temperature changes.* You feel hot, your face goes red, your palms become clammy, and you may start to sweat. Or it may be the opposite: you go cold.

These symptoms are all signs that your body's 'fight or flight' response has kicked in. This is your body's instinctive response to any threat – physical or psychological, real or imagined. Once a threat is registered, your brain puts your body on red alert, by sending signals to the glands near the kidneys to release adrenaline, a hormone that gears up your body with the strength and energy to either fight the threat or turn on your heels and scarper.

Next time you notice you are starting to feel anxious, try to sit quietly and, if you can, close your eyes. See if you can slow your breathing and focus on the breath going in and out of your nostrils. Now, turn your mental focus into your body. Imagine there's a remote control robot trawling your body, recording physical sensations. What does it pick up and where? If you can, give each sensation a rating of between 0 and 10 depending on how strong it is (10 being strongest). For example, neck tension 8; headache 9; stomach-churning 3.

Step 2: Pick up on themes

When self-doubt emerges and you start to feel anxious about what might happen, the precise thoughts or images that come into your head are unique and personal to you. You may find it hard to imagine that anyone else feels the same. In a way, you're right – your anxious predictions are unique, shaped by a combination of the experiences that created your Bottom Line, and the nature of the Bottom Line itself. However, there are certain themes that come up again and again when people feel anxious and uncertain. Here are the most common – see if you can spot yours.

- *You overestimate the chances that something bad will happen.*

You are absolutely convinced that it's highly likely that something will go wrong, without any evidence to support your prediction. When Tara imagines spending an evening with people she knows, she overestimates the likelihood of excruciating silences and frosty exchanges. She takes no account of the evidence, that if people are friendly and easy to talk to at work or the playground, chances are they'll be the same elsewhere.

- *You overestimate how bad it will be if something bad does happen.*

When your mind is in anxious prediction mode, it doesn't think rationally. So you're unlikely to assume that, if something bad does happen, it will be over in moments and quickly forgotten about. Tara can't imagine that if a dinner party turns out to be dull, then that's all it would be – an evening when everyone starts yawning, looking at their watch, and calling a taxi at 10.30 p.m. She imagines that it would permanently change her relationship with the friend who invited her, that the friend would somehow blame her for not being 'entertaining' enough, and would tell everyone at work how dull she is. Her colleagues would start to avoid her.

- *You underestimate your ability to cope.*

Not only do you assume the worst will happen, you're also convinced that there will be nothing you can do to improve the situation or make it more bearable. It doesn't occur to Tara that if there were some awkward silences, she might think of something to say that would get the conversation going again, or, if it was an awful evening, she could simply turn it into a funny story to tell her sister later.

- *You underestimate other people.*

You may also discount external things that might improve or even defuse the situation entirely. Tara, for example, overlooks the fact that there would be other people present, all hoping to have an enjoyable time. So the success of the evening wouldn't be her sole responsibility.

Step 3: Spot avoidance tactics or safety-seeking behaviours

When you're faced with a threat, it makes sense to get out of the way. Tara makes up fairly complex excuses to *avoid* group social events and then often overcompensates by sending the host flowers as an apology. This can prove expensive, and Tara feels as if she's tying herself in knots with the stories she's telling people. Still, it's worth it for the relief she feels at not having to turn up. If, for some reason, she can't get out of it, she goes into *safety-seeking* mode with her 'life and soul' routine. She can't just relax, go with the flow, and be her natural self.

So what do you do when you feel threatened? Do you avoid the threat altogether, or do you take precautions to protect yourself in case it comes true? If you take precautions, what are they? Might they in fact turn out to be unnecessary? If you're not sure what you do, next time you feel your anxiety signals kick in, try to notice what runs through your mind. Watch your behaviour when you're in the situation as well – what do you notice yourself doing (or deliberately not doing) in order to keep yourself safe? For further guidance on how to manage anxiety, read the rest of the chapter, then complete the following Anxiety reality-check worksheet.

🖋 TIME TO GET WRITING:

Your reactions to anxiety

Have a look at the following **Anxiety reality-check worksheet** on pages 72 and 73. To give you an idea of the kind of things to record, you'll find a sheet filled in by Tara on pages 88–9. The worksheet is designed to help you tune into what happens when anxious predictions emerge, and to begin to work with them and undermine their influence on your life. Remember, worksheets on which you record day-to-day experiences are a powerful means of helping you to change – often more so than just doing it all in your head, or writing things down in a journal or diary. Worksheets encourage you to investigate carefully the step-by-step process that keeps your low self-esteem alive – to see the system in operation as it happens, rather than just thinking about it in general terms.

Anxiety reality-check worksheet

Aim to fill in the worksheet as close as possible to the time you actually experience the anxiety. This is for several reasons. It can be difficult to tune into anxious predictions when everything is normal and relaxed. When you look back 'cold' on a situation, your thoughts and the precautions you took can make you cringe so you feel reluctant to record them honestly. And the longer you wait to record an event, the less detail you remember. Filling in a structured sheet may seem hard work to start with, but it's worth giving it a try. Closely observing your reactions in this way may help you identify the very earliest warning signals of anxiety, so you can learn how to intervene before your anxiety takes hold.

Here's what you'll be recording:

Day, date and time. When did you experience the anxiety symptoms? People who have filled in these charts for a week or two often spot patterns to their anxiety. For example, they find it starts at a certain time of day (e.g. first thing in the morning) or at a certain point in the week (e.g. Friday evening).

The situation. Anxiety-triggers can be external (e.g. a disagreement with a work colleague) or internal one (e.g.

Anxiety reality-check worksheet

Day/Date/Time	Situation	Emotions and body sensations (Rate intensity from 0 to 10)	Anxious predictions (Rate belief from 0 to 10)	Avoidance/precautions	Alternative scenarios Use the key questions to find other views of the situation. (Rate feelings of relief they produce from 0 to 10)	Experiment 1 What did you do instead of taking your usual precautions? 2 What were the results?

imagining your boss being displeased with the report you just finished). Make a note of exactly where you were, who you were with, and what you were doing or thinking about.

Your emotions. Were you feeling panic, pressure, irritation, frustration, embarrassment, despair? Jot them down. Then give each one an 'intensity rating' between 0 and 10, depending on how strong they are, with 10 being as strong as it could possibly be, 5 being moderately strong, 2 being a slight emotion, and so on. Rating your emotions helps you attune your mental antenna, so you can learn to pick up these cues earlier and earlier.

Sensations in your body. Were you shaky, or beginning to feel hot? Could you feel yourself starting to clench your jaw? Was your stomach churning? In Step 1 you noted how varied the bodily sensations can be when anxious predictions kick in. Note down all the sensations you were aware of, then give them a rating as you did with your emotions, between 0 and 10, with 0 being least strong and 10 being strongest.

Your anxious predictions. Write down your thoughts about what you thought would go wrong. Then rate each prediction between 0 and 10 depending on how strongly you believed it: 10 means you were strongly convinced, with no shadow of doubt; 5 means you were in two minds; 1 means it was a remote possibility. You'll probably find that the more strongly you believed your predictions, the more anxious you felt. You may even have experienced vivid and convincing images of your anxious predictions coming true, like watching a film in your mind's eye.

On the other hand, you may find your predictions are not so much statements or images of what you fear might happen, but rather short phrases such as 'Here I go again!' or questions such as 'What if I can't cope?' or 'Will they like me?' Write them down and then spend a little time considering what they mean. If short phrases have come up, see if you can 'unpack' them. What fears might they represent? What do they suggest might be about to happen? If your predictions take the form of questions, search out the prediction hiding behind the question. Ask yourself: what is the answer to this question which would account for the *anxiety* I'm experiencing? After all, if your question was 'Will I be able to do it?' but your answer to this was 'Yes, I will,' you wouldn't be feeling anxious. The hidden prediction that makes sense of how you feel is, 'I won't be able to do it.' Once you've unpacked the meaning behind these statements, rate how strongly you believe them, from 0 to 10.

Your actions: avoidance or precautions. What do you do to avoid the threat and keep yourself safe? Complete avoidance is usually relatively easy to spot (e.g. in Tara's case, she turns down the majority of social invitations that come her way). Other self-protective manoeuvres may be less obvious. For example, when Tara can't escape a social engagement, another of her strategies (besides making huge efforts to be entertaining) is to focus the conversation on the other person, and say as little as possible about herself. Your precautions may be so subtle that you are not fully aware of them, but by careful observation and keeping a record of as many examples as you can over a week or so you may be able to pick up a pattern. In particular, watch out for the feeling that you've had a narrow escape – this feeling is often a sign that unnecessary precautions are around.

Step 4: Look for alternative scenarios

Once you have a clear picture of your anxious predictions in a range of different situations, it's time to learn how to question their validity rather than automatically reacting as if they were true. Experimenting with putting these new ideas into practice will then help to make them real. Remember, anxious predictions keep the vicious circle of low self-confidence going. Coming up with alternatives to your predictions will help reduce the fear in your life. It's a crucial step in helping you experience life as your true self, boosting your confidence and your enjoyment of everyday living. Once again, your best bet is to work on specific examples, rather than addressing your fears on an abstract, general level – you'll get more mileage out of the process that way.

You may find the key questions below will help you rethink your usual perspective. On your worksheet, write down the answers that spring to mind and rate how far you believe each one from 0 to 10. It's OK if you don't fully believe your alternatives to start with – by the time you've had a chance to try them out in real life, they should more convincing. If this doesn't happen, maybe the answers you've come up with are not the ones that will make a difference to you. So have another go at coming up with alternatives. Remember, your aim is to feel less anxious and more able to change the way you act in situations where you experience self-doubt.

Key questions

What makes you think what you do? Have experiences in your past led you to expect disaster in the present day? Has it simply become a habit – in this situation, you automatically assume things will go wrong? Or are your thoughts driven by your moods or emotions?

What do the *facts* of the situation tell you? Looking as objectively as you can at the situation, are you overlooking evidence that suggests things might not go as badly as you fear? Have you had any experiences of similar situations in the past that didn't end in disaster, for instance? Are you ignoring help from people or other sources that would make a difference? Is there anything else you've been ignoring or discounting which would suggest that your fears may be exaggerated?

Could you view the situation in a different way? What would you say to a friend who came to you with the same fears and concerns – would you agree that things are likely to go wrong for them? Or would you reassure them that in all probability things will be just fine, or if they do go wrong, it won't be the end of the world? Remember, there are many ways of thinking about an experience. You may view your mistakes as disasters or evidence of predictable failure, but another person might view them as perfectly understandable under the circumstances, or as something useful to learn from. Or they might not even notice them at all. So ask yourself, are you exaggerating the *importance* of the situation? What would your view of it be, for example, if your mood was more buoyant, and you were feeling at your most confident and optimistic about life? Can you picture how you'll feel about this event in a month, a year or ten years? Will you even remember what happened? And if so, will you still feel the same about it? Write down the new perspectives you've found, and rate how far you believe each of them (0 to10). You don't have to be fully convinced that your new take on things is true, but make sure it fits the facts. If it's not at all believable, it's no real use to you.

What is the *worst* that could happen? Writing down your worst fears can be an instant reality-check – once they're on paper, you can see how detached from reality they really are. Tara had a clear vision of a totally silent dinner party where the other guests looked scornfully at her but the truth is that few adults would act so maliciously.

What is the *best* that could happen? Now think of the opposite to the above – what would be the best possible outcome? Try to think of a scenario at the other end of the scale from the worst scenario. For this exercise, Tara imagined a dinner party where she had everyone enthralled, hanging on her every word, and making them weep with laughter. At the end, every guest hugged her and told her she was the most interesting and entertaining person they had ever met. She had no problem seeing how unrealistic and ridiculous this vision was. But it also helped her see that her negative predictions were just as exaggerated.

Realistically, what is the *most likely* to happen? Once you've imagined your worst and best scenarios, can you see that realistically, the most likely outcome is probably somewhere in between? Write down what that might be. For Tara, it's that the evening is perfectly pleasant, conversation flows easily and, by the end of the evening, people feel relaxed and comfortable in each other's company. She hasn't been the life and soul of the party, but she's contributed to the conversation and told a couple of stories that have made people laugh. She's got to know the other guests a bit better, decided there's a couple of them that she really likes, and, overall, enjoyed the evening.

What's your emergency strategy? If the worst did happen, what could you do about it? In your moments of doubt and anxious predictions, you tend to underestimate – or completely overlook – your ability to cope. But the likelihood is that you could actually deal with the situation perfectly well. If Tara, for example, did end up at a dinner party where another guest took a dislike to her, and started making challenging or disparaging comments, it's likely she could stand up for herself. She knows she's perfectly capable of fighting her corner when she's challenged in a work meeting. It's also likely that the other guests would intervene and tell the rude person to 'back off' or suggest they've had too much to drink.

It can be very reassuring to formulate a detailed plan for what you'd do if your fears did come true. After all, once you've worked out how to cope with the worst-case scenario, everything else is a walk in the park! If you've successfully dealt with a similar situation in the past, what could you learn from this? What would you do again? What aspects of your personality could be useful? (Sense of humour, ability to appear calm, your methodical or ordered way of thinking?) What support could you draw on from those around you? Knowledge is power – what information could you get in advance to help you deal more effectively with the situation?

Thinking long-term, are there any changes you can put in place now to make your worst-case scenario less of a nightmare? Do you need to start managing someone's unreasonable expectations of you, or start asking for more help and support? If your worst-case scenario is missing a crucial work deadline, do you need to talk to your boss now about spreading the workload or readjusting the schedule? OK, it may not be easy for you to do this – you may find such changes initially create more negative predictions (you imagine your boss will be angry with you or start to question your ability). You may also find it triggers a self-critical commentary – 'But I should be able to cope alone'. If so, make a note of these thoughts and search for alternatives to them. They, too, can be questioned and tested out. Your boss may already have an idea that the deadline is unrealistic and the workload too much for one person, and welcome the heads-up while it's still possible to salvage the situation.

And bear in mind that even if the situation truly can't be changed, you can learn to change how you think and feel about it – that's the point of this exercise.

Step 5: Time to check it out – experiment!

There's a reason that so many confidence-building courses involve something challenging like abseiling, rock climbing or completing a high ropes course. It's a powerful way to show you that no matter how loud and convincing your brain's fear messages may be ('I'll fall off', 'That can't be safe', 'I'm going to die'), it doesn't mean they're right. By screwing up your courage and completing the challenge, you get a new set of messages – 'The safety harness held', 'The instructors knew exactly what they were doing', 'It was safe', 'My body was strong enough to hold my weight', 'I could keep my balance'. You may even decide you enjoyed it or found it exhilarating. But unless you'd had that experience for yourself, a part of you would remain unconvinced that you could complete the challenge safely, even if you watched other people doing it and told yourself that, logically, you'd be safe too.

This is why acting on your new predictions is so important. By physically experiencing them for yourself, you build up the most convincing evidence to contradict your original fearful predictions and support your new, more balanced perspective. Experimenting with acting differently gives you a chance to find out for yourself if the alternatives you have thought up are in line with the facts and therefore helpful to you, or whether you need to think again.

Do as you've always done, and you'll get what you always get, so the saying goes. It's become a bit of a cliché, but it contains an essential truth. Plans and good intentions only go so far – to change the habits of a lifetime, you have to walk the talk!

We know that facing the very situations you've been avoiding, and dropping all your normal self-protective measures, can feel just as terrifying as abseiling over the side of a cliff. After all, you're deliberately pushing yourself way out of your comfort zone. But there's no way round it – experiments turn abstract ideas into concrete reality, something that you can believe at gut level. Jumping off the cliff and abseiling down it is the most effective way of convincing yourself that you can survive the experiment – and even possibly enjoy it!

Of course, your experiments don't have to involve cliffs, or even be dramatic in any way. They can be small tests, planned to fit into daily events (for example, planning to say something in the first five minutes of your meeting tomorrow). You could also use situations that arise naturally (for example, experimenting with saying, 'I'll have to look at my schedule and get back to you on that,' instead of an automatic 'OK' the next time someone asks you to volunteer for extra work). Or you could go for a mix of both. Whichever you choose, you'll get the most out of your experiments if you record the details in your **Anxiety reality-check worksheet**.

The idea of setting up an experiment may feel artificial, or just plain weird. But it really does work! And it's easier than you might think if you follow these three simple steps:

1 Pin down the details!

You can't test a vague feeling or intuition (such as 'Things

will go badly', or 'I will mess up'). If there are no specif-
ics, how will you know whether or not they have come
true? You need details! So write down exactly what you
expect to happen, and how you think you will act and feel.
Include, if relevant, how you think you and other people
will also react. If you predict people will disapprove of
you, work out how you would know this was happening.
What would they say or do that would tell you that they
were indeed disapproving? Would they turn their back
on you mid-conversation, or roll their eyes, muttering
'Good grief!' under their breath? Once you have defined
how you would know what you fear is happening, you
will know exactly what to look for when you go into the
situation. Then you need to rate each prediction according to how strongly you believe it, on a scale of 0 to 10.
For example, if one of your predictions is that you will
feel so nervous you won't be able to cope, rate how far
you believe this to be true. You could also give a 0–10 rating to just how nervous you predict you will be – 9 or
10 perhaps. Many people are surprised to find that while
they did feel nervous, it wasn't as intense as they expected
– more like a 4 or 5. Rating your predicted feelings gives
you an objective way to check out if things are as bad as
you anticipate.

2 Drop your precautions

You should have a good idea of your usual precautions
by now – the things you do to make yourself feel safer
when you're in the grip of anxious predictions. But this
experiment only works if you drop them. When you were
learning to swim, you'd never have found out that you
could stay afloat unaided if you hadn't taken off your
buoyancy aid. You might have felt frightened the first time

your swimming teacher or parent persuaded you to ven-
ture into the pool without it. But if you didn't sink, and
you got yourself from one side of the pool to the other, you
learned something valuable from that experience – that
you could swim. And you updated your self-image from
'non-swimmer' to 'swimmer'.

Think of all the things you might be tempted to do in
self-protection, no matter how small. Plan in advance
what you will do instead. For example, if your experiment
involves going to a party, and your normal strategy would
be to hide in the kitchen all night, doing the washing up
and getting people drinks and snacks, so that no one finds
out how 'boring' you are, then you might plan to limit your
'helping' time to 30 minutes, and spend the rest of the event
mingling with other guests (without handing out snacks or
offering to refresh their glass!). Or if you never admit when
you're annoyed or hurt by your partner, because you're
afraid you'll be rejected if you show your real feelings, try
being a bit more open about your negative as well as your
positive emotions, (For example, next time they come in
late, plan what you'll say: 'I felt so worried last night when
you stayed out late and didn't call that I couldn't sleep.')

3 Review your results

Remember, this experiment is a personal learning experience – not a test that you pass or fail. It may go one of
two ways, and both are equally valuable sources of information. So don't be reluctant to record the details if you
think it didn't go well. The more you notice and reflect on
what happened, the more useful this exercise will be. Use
the final column of your worksheet to jot down what happened. Then, describe how you felt, and what you learned
from it. Ask yourself what it says about your negative view

of yourself, and whether it suggests you need to update your self-image.

In an ideal world, your experiment will show you that your anxious predictions were *not* correct, and that the alternative scenarios that you wrote down in your chart were indeed more in touch with reality. However, you may find your anxious predictions were accurate. This can feel devastating and it's crucial not to turn this minor setback into a reason to give up. You may feel low or discouraged, but if you can, try to distance yourself from those emotions. As you know by now, it's hard to think objectively when your mind has switched on its 'negative-thinking' radar. When you're back in a place you feel safe, and have given yourself time to calm down, then try to appraise the situation and assess how it came about. Was it in fact nothing to do with you, but caused by something else within the situation? (For example, if you spoke up at the meeting only to have someone immediately talk over you, does that say more about the other person than you? Does that person regularly talk over whoever is speaking in meetings?) Look for other explanations for what went wrong, besides you. If you started up a conversation with a stranger at a party that was rather stilted, could that be simply because you didn't have much in common, rather than the fact that you're boring? If you're convinced that you did contribute in some way to what happened, don't give yourself a hard time. Be kind to yourself and focus on learning from it – how could you handle the situation differently in the future to change the end result? Be honest – did you drop all of your precautions? Did you really take off those armbands and jump in at the deep end? Did you lurk in the kitchen at the party, and only come out when most people were ready to go home and not in the mood for striking up new conversations? Did you concede the floor when you were interrupted in the meeting rather than saying, 'Let me finish my point'? Do you notice that 'Phew, I made it' feeling that tells you safety-seeking behaviours are still around? If so what could you do differently next time?

Here's how Tara embarked on this experiment.

Tara's experiment

Six months ago, a work colleague asked Tara to join their book group. She loved reading so the idea instantly appealed to her. But the thought of actually turning up and attending the group made her feel extremely anxious. She had a clear vision of the group turning to look frostily at her when she arrived, someone piping up, 'Who invited her?' and there not being any space for her to sit down. She then imagined herself red in the face and too intimidated to speak up, so that by the end of the evening everyone would assume she was boring, hadn't read the book or had nothing to say. At work, no one would mention the date of the next meeting. Some of these predictions felt more believable than others: on a scale of 0 to 10, she rated the prediction she'd go red as a 9, and the prediction of someone whispering 'Who invited her?' as a 5.

Tara tried a mini experiment earlier in the week by agreeing to go for coffee with a group of friends. She'd predicted that she'd have nothing to say, and would sit there smiling dumbly while clever banter went on around her. In reality, people weren't trying to be especially clever or funny, they were just talking about everyday things, such as what their kids were up to, and where they planned to go on holiday this year. Tara soon found herself relaxing, and, when she spoke, people listened, smiled, responded and seemed interested.

She decided to approach the colleague who'd originally asked her about the book group to find out the date of the next meeting and ask if it would be OK if she came along. The colleague seemed delighted, and told her the date of the meeting, and the book they'd be discussing. The group took it in turns to meet at each other's houses, and would bring a bottle of wine and some nibbles. The book was actually one that Tara had already read and really loved. So she got out her copy at home and read it again, with pleasure. She was tempted to make notes on things she could say about it, but realised this would be a precaution. The best experiment would be not to over-prepare, but to go along and say whatever came into her head. She also made what might be a more accurate prediction of what would happen, that she would go along, people would be friendly, she might feel a bit shy and not say a lot, but no one would ridicule her.

As she predicted, people were very friendly when she went along, and made her feel welcome. And far from having nothing to say, Tara found herself joining in with the lively discussion – when she talked, she noticed people really listened to her and she could see a couple of people nodding in agreement. She noticed that two of the group members hadn't managed to finish the book, so didn't have as much to contribute, but there seemed to be an understanding that everyone was busy and if you didn't manage to finish the book, it was still OK to come along. After a while, the talk turned to general chat and Tara got on really well with the woman sitting next to her. She left the evening feeling elated, and made a decision to do a similar experiment the next time she found herself making anxious predictions, instead of allowing them to go on ruling her life.

Now give yourself a pat on the back

If you've done your experiment, congratulations – that took real courage, however it turned out. Give yourself a pat on the back for facing the challenge. Now, what have you learned about yourself, other people and your relationships with them? Would it be most useful to repeat the experiment, so as to build your confidence in the results and in yourself? Or is it time to try similar changes in a new or perhaps more challenging situation? What's your next step?

ESSENTIAL TAKE-HOME MESSAGES FROM THIS CHAPTER

- When you feel as if your personal Rules might be broken, your mind fills with doubts, and you feel under threat. Symptoms of anxiety follow and you start creating fearful scenarios in your mind, imagining all the ways that things could go wrong.
- Anxiety and self-doubt affect your ability to think rationally – as well as overestimating the chances that something will go wrong, you disregard or underestimate your ability to cope and handle the situation.
- You then take precautions to stop the worst from happening. If they work, in the short-term, you'll feel as if you had a narrow escape. But in the end, precautions hold you back. They make it impossible to find out and experience for yourself that your anxious predictions were incorrect. Your fears and doubts persist, only to come back into your life another day.
- If you want to break free from the tyranny of this kind of thinking, and break the vicious circle that stops your natural self-confidence from blossoming,

Tara's Anxiety reality-check worksheet

Day/Date/Time	Situation	Emotions and body sensations (Rate intensity from 0 to10)	Anxious predictions (Rate belief from 0 to 10)	Avoidance/precautions	Alternative scenarios Use the key questions to find other views of the situation. (Rate feelings of relief they produce from 0 to 10)	Experiment 1 What did you do instead of taking your usual precautions? 2 What were the results?
Monday 10th Jan 2.30 p.m.	Considering going to book club	Anxious 8 Heart pounding 7 Face getting hot 6 Stomach churning 7	The room will fall silent when I walk in 7 I'll go red 9 Someone will whisper 'Who invited her?' 5 I will be tongue-tied and clam up 9	Usually turn down this kind of invitation. If I do go, try to be very entertaining. Or try not to talk about myself.	People will carry on chatting when I walk in, the host will get up to greet me 10 People will be pleased to see me and make me feel welcome 10 I may be quiet at first but maybe able to contribute something by the end of the evening 7	1 Went along to the book group 2 I really enjoyed it! Had lots to say, people listened and I felt relaxed and accepted. Decided I would go again

If they're rude to me, I will know that it's not the sort of book group I want to join **5**

I will feel so uncomfortable I'll want to run out of the room **8** you need to learn to spot the early warning signs that you're going into 'anxious prediction mode'. Your clues are the physical and emotional changes triggered by anxiety.

- You can learn to question your fearful predictions and find it easier to come up with alternative scenarios that are more realistic. If you experiment with trying out these new perspectives and facing situations you normally avoid, dropping your usual precautions, you will discover for yourself whether your predictions are accurate or whether in fact your fresh perspective matches the situation better than your old one.

Life Lesson

Filling out structured worksheets about your feelings may feel artificial but it will help you follow things through in a systematic way rather than getting stuck.

5

CHALLENGING YOUR INNER CRITIC

You're useless, you've messed up again, you're fat and greedy, you're pathetic, you're weak, you're an embarrassment, you're a failure at everything, why do you even bother, you made a fool of yourself again, everyone was laughing at you, why would he want to go out with *you*? Could you imagine saying those things to a friend? Yet, chances are, you say something similar to yourself on a daily basis.

People who lack self-confidence tend to have a very vocal inner critic and self-criticism can be almost second nature. Ridiculing yourself, putting yourself down, calling yourself names, pointing out every little thing that goes wrong, is an ingrained habit that switches on the moment you get up. At times, the volume can be turned low on your inner critic, but it's rarely switched off altogether.

Your mind is tuned in to pick up every little mistake or setback, and you use this as the basis to completely dismiss yourself as a person – 'you're stupid', 'you're ugly', 'you're a bad mother', 'you're weak'. Your wonky thinking homes in on the negative like a heat-seeking missile and completely ignores anything positive. Small triumphs and achievements are either unacknowledged or played down – 'it was luck', 'it was nothing'.

Self-critical thoughts pack a powerful emotional punch. If a friend stood next to you and berated you for being a pathetic waste of space, you'd expect to feel low or anxious. But the brain doesn't differentiate between messages received from external and from internal sources, so that your own critical tirade has exactly the same effect on your emotions.

Not convinced? Try this quick experiment. Read the following list of words slowly and carefully, really allowing them to sink in. Imagine they apply to you. Then notice the impact on your confidence and mood.

Lazy	Ugly	Misfit
Loser	Irritating	Reject
Pathetic	Repulsive	Stupid
Dumb	Inferior	Worthless

Some of the words may be part of your personal repertoire of put-downs. If so, underline them. Then jot down any other words that feature regularly. These are the words you need to watch out for.

A crucial step in moving towards a more balanced and accepting view of yourself is learning to notice when you are being self-critical. You'll need to observe carefully the impact that self-criticism has on your feelings and how you operate in day-to-day situations.

In this chapter, you will learn how to . . .

- Let go of the belief that self-criticism is useful or serves a purpose (such as motivating you, or keeping you from making a fool of yourself).

- Become aware of subtle, ingrained self-critical thinking.
- Question self-critical thoughts and spot biased thinking patterns.

FIVE REASONS YOUR INNER CRITIC IS NOT YOUR FRIEND!

Do you suspect that without your self-critical voice picking up on your faults, you'd never have got anywhere in life? Do you think it stops you resting on your laurels, or getting lazy? Do you secretly worry that if you start to congratulate yourself, and think all the time about what went well, you'll become a bit smug and complacent? In some cultures and families, there's a belief that thinking well of yourself leads to 'big-headedness', and that the best way to motivate someone to do better is to pick out their faults, not point out what they did well. Or you may think that your self-critical thinking is the only thing that stops you making a complete fool of yourself, or getting hurt or rejected in personal relationships. The truth is, self-critical thinking does the opposite of motivating and protecting you. You've got where you have in life *in spite of* it, not because of it. Here are the five ways your critical voice stops you from achieving your true potential, and stands in the way of self-acceptance and a more fulfilling life.

1 It's not on your side

Your inner critic likes to hold up a magnifying glass to the slightest fault, mistake or element of self-doubt. When it finds one, it uses that fault as a reason to condemn you as a whole person, writing you off as a pathetic loser. Would you tolerate this from a friend? Would you choose to spend time with someone who tells you that the reason you forgot it was 'no-uniform day' at your children's school is because you're a useless airhead who can't get anything right?

Your inner critic never uses that magnifying glass to highlight what you've done well, or your assets and strengths. Just like every other person on this planet, you're a mix of good and bad, strengths and weaknesses, talents and flaws. But your inner critic edits out your good points and is ready to condemn you on the basis of the smallest mistake or slip-up. Imagine working for a boss like this! How long would you last before you resigned, or at least started looking for another job? A week? A month? Six months? Yet many of us have put up with a raging inner critic for years.

2 It holds you back

Imagine you have a seven-year-old son and he decides he wants to learn to play cricket. You have a choice of two local clubs to send him to – one that's run by Jeff, and one that's run by Neil. Jeff never lets up on any boy – he's always on their case, telling them what went wrong, picking out every tiny mistake. He's a stickler for detail. He regularly gives the team a dressing down for general behaviour, for being lazy and unfocused. He believes that if he lets go of his tight rein even for a second, the boys will start to slack off. Neil, on the other hand, believes in positive encouragement. He points out what went well before he talks about where there's room for improvement. He has a knack of noticing a particular talent in every boy, and helping them make the most of it. He believes in regular pep talks and thinks boosting the boys' confidence is the key to keeping them motivated. Now, which of the teams would you send your seven-year-old to? Which approach would you imagine would bring out the best in him, and nurture his enthusiasm?

Most people learn more when their successes are rewarded, praised and encouraged than when they are criticised and punished for their failures. Imagine what *you* could achieve if you didn't have that negative 'coach' continually telling you that you could have done something better, faster, more effectively. Do you think that being told you're lazy, pathetic, or just hopeless, inspires you to take risks, make changes and try new things? Or do you think it holds you back?

3 It blocks learning

Far from helping you to overcome problems, your inner critic prevents you from thinking clearly about yourself and your life. As well as zapping your motivation and making you feel discouraged, it prevents you from taking the 'objective' view you need to learn from your mistakes. By discounting your successes, and magnifying every mistake or problem, you lose the opportunity to learn from what went right, and get a clear and constructive view of what you genuinely need to change.

4 It pipes up when you're low

Not only does your inner critic lower your mood and make you more prone to depression, anxiety or lack of confidence, it follows up by criticising you for feeling this way, telling you that you're pathetic for feeling afraid, or that you're weak or just feeling sorry for yourself. It makes you feel ashamed for feeling these things, or feel that there's something wrong with you.

There's still a lot of stigma attached to anxiety and depression but the truth is that they are very common conditions, and can be seen as an almost inevitable reaction to certain life experiences. They can easily be caused by stressful events, relationship problems or childhood issues. You're certainly not the first person to feel this way and you won't be the last. It is possible to overcome anxiety and depression, and reading this book and following the exercises will help you do that. You won't overcome them by criticising yourself for having problems and difficulties, or telling yourself to 'pull yourself together'!

5 It lies to you

When things go wrong, in addition to criticising yourself for what you did, you probably tell yourself you should have acted differently. Perhaps you're right in thinking that acting differently would have been in your best interests. But in reality, chances are you had good reasons for acting as you did, even if in the end your course of action turned out to be misguided. (Maybe you were feeling stressed or tired or had too much on your mind, maybe you didn't have the help you needed, or were misinformed about a situation.) Your critical inner voice lies to you and tells you that it was obvious what you should have done, and the only reason you couldn't see that was because you're just so stupid. By blocking your ability to see a situation objectively, and using any setback as a stick to beat you with, your inner critic is stopping you learning from the situation and moving on.

HOW TO SPOT SELF-CRITICAL THINKING

Sometimes self-critical thinking is loud and clear, like a foghorn in your head. But it's not always this obvious, and it may be the quieter, more insidious running commentary that does the most damage. If you've been lacking in self-confidence for some time, you may have become so used to your self-critical voice that you barely even register that it's there any more – but the messages still get through.

Consciously focusing your awareness on your critical thoughts may seem counter-intuitive – you're turning the spotlight on what makes you feel bad. But in fact you can only defuse the power your inner critic has over your self-image by becoming familiar with how self-criticism operates.

The biggest sign that your inner critic is in operation is a change in your emotional state. Unlike your anxious predictions, which are most likely to trigger fear, apprehension, panic or anxiety, your inner critic will make you feel any of these emotions:

Guilty	Ashamed
Sad	Embarrassed
Disappointed in yourself	Angry with yourself
Frustrated	Depressed
Hopeless	Despairing

✎ TIME TO GET WRITING:

Spotting your own self-critical thoughts

It can take time to find the strength and conviction to eliminate a toxic relationship from your life. But hopefully, you won't need any more convincing that there are no plus-sides to your inner critic. Those self-critical thoughts of yours have nothing positive to bring to your life, so it's time to show them the door, once and for all. But before you do, you're going to interrogate them! After all, you've put up with this nasty tirade for long enough, you deserve to learn something from your inner critic before you eliminate it.

The aim of the next exercise is to find a way of listening to your inner critic, *without* getting sucked in to the usual negative cycle of emotion-and-behaviour that it can trigger. It will help you look as objectively as you can at the words, feelings, sentiments or images that come up time and again, then scratch the surface and see what's lurking beneath them.

The **Inner critic worksheet** on pages 100–1 will help you do this. You may be tempted to simply write down your self-critical thoughts in a diary, but this can in fact make you feel worse. Using the worksheet will help keep you focused and maintain a degree of objectivity. Hopefully, doing this exercise will raise awareness and put an 'early warning' system in place so you can nip self-critical thoughts in the bud in future. A lot of the time, the self-critical voice has unleashed a lengthy tirade before we even register the fact that it's talking. Not only will filling in the sheet throw a spotlight on exactly what is running through your mind when you feel bad about yourself, you'll also understand more clearly how these thoughts affect your life, and how they keep your self-confidence suppressed.

It may seem a daunting task, but you should start to see results fairly quickly. After filling in the worksheet for a few days, you should notice you're more sensitive to the changes in your feelings, and to the self-critical thoughts that spark them off. You can begin to step back from these thoughts and see them for what they really are – an opinion or an old thinking habit, not a reflection of the person you really are.

Bear in mind that self-critical thoughts are powerful because they've got a direct line to your Bottom Line – your deepest beliefs about yourself. The worksheet structure goes some way to disabling this power, allowing you to examine your beliefs safely. It's a bit like putting them behind a glass screen so you can examine them in safety.

HOW TO DO IT

If possible, write down your self-critical thoughts as soon as they occur – the longer you leave it, the harder it may be to recall them in helpful detail. Here's what to fill in:

1 Date, day and time

Record when you felt bad about yourself. It may help you see if there are any patterns over time.

2 What was happening

Record as much detail as you can about what was happening at the moment you began to feel bad. Where were you? Who were you with? What were you doing? Jot down briefly what was going on. You may actually not have been doing anything in particular (e.g. 'in the shower'; 'washing up') and what brought on the self-critical thinking was not the situation but something you mind was dwelling on. If that's the case, put down the general idea you were focusing on (e.g. 'Thinking about talking to the neighbours about their tree' or 'Replaying my latest argument with Mum'.)

3 How you felt

Record your emotions and body sensations. It could be just one main emotion (e.g. embarrassment) or a mixture of emotions (e.g. embarrassment, shame, depression). What, if any, physical sensations did you have (e.g. a headache;

Inner critic worksheet

Day/ Date/ Time	What is happening	How I feel: emotions & sensations *(Rate each, 0 to10)*	What I'm thinking *(Rate belief in each thought, 0 to 10)*	Knee-jerk reactions	My shiny new thoughts! Use the five 'power questions' to find other perspectives on your thoughts. *(Rate belief in each new perspective, 0 to 10)*	EBA a) **Emotions** How I feel, with my shiny new thoughts. *(Rate each feeling, 0 to10 for intensity)* b) **Believability** How much I now believe my self-critical thoughts. *(Rate each thought for believability, 0 to10)* c) **Actions** What can I do? Experiments.

tension in the head, neck or jaw; a sinking feeling in the stomach). Write down each emotion and physical sensation, giving it a rating of between 0 and 10 according to how strong it felt. A rating of 1 or 2 would mean just a slight emotional reaction or physical sensation; a rating of 5 would mean a moderate amount of distress; and a rating of 10 would mean the emotion or sensation was as bad as it could be.

4 What you thought

Self-critical thoughts come in many forms. Some are like a running commentary or nagging voice in the brain. If you can, write down the words, phrases or sentences word-for-word or as close as you can get to them. And your inner critic has other ways of undermining you. It can create silent images in your mind's eye, often snapshots from your past (a teacher frowning with impatience while you answered a question in class). Describe the image and try to decode its message – e.g. 'you're irritating', 'you don't understand what you're talking about'.

There may be times when you feel upset but you can't pin down any particular thoughts or images. Your self-critical voice is there, it's just working subconsciously. Can you try to strip away the layers and find out what message you've taken from the situation? For example, a friend isn't returning your phone calls – you're feeling low and uneasy and not sure why. Could your inner critic be saying she's realised how unadventurous you really are, so she's trying to distance herself from you? Hearing about a colleague's promotion may make you feel hopeless – is your inner critic inferring that the post wasn't offered to you because you're just not clever enough to go further up the ladder? Write down the details of the situation and any insights you have into the critical messages it conveys.

If you can, give each self-critical thought, image or meaning a rating of between 0 and 10 to reflect how convinced you are that the criticism is real or justified – how much you believe it.

5 Knee-jerk reactions

It's hard to remain immune to the emotions stirred up by your inner critic. On a good day, when you're feeling robust and upbeat, you might be able to put aside a momentary mental snipe and get on with your day. But a longer tirade is more difficult to ignore, especially if you're already feeling vulnerable. Write down what you did when your inner critic piped up – did you head straight for the biscuit barrel or reach for the corkscrew? Did you retreat into your shell and not say much for the rest of the day? Did you apologise when you didn't need to, or try to overcompensate by working harder or longer hours? Did you allow someone to walk all over you?

Top tips for making this work

- **Do it every day.** Note down one or two examples a day for as long as it takes for you to gain an understanding – it may take you a couple of days or a couple of weeks, depending on how subtle your self-critical messages are.

- **Write it as it happens.** Try to write down your thoughts as soon as they occur. You'll need to keep your worksheet with you for a few days. That's because even though self-critical thoughts can have a very powerful effect at the time, afterwards you may not remember exactly what was going through your mind. If you're in a situation where you can't do this, try to jot down some notes on whatever piece of paper you have to hand, or on your phone or laptop, and write them up in detail the first opportunity you get.

- **Beware of excuses.** Focusing on upsetting ideas wouldn't be most people's top choice of leisure activity! So a bit of procrastination or avoidance tactics are only to be expected. But once you've tidied that sock drawer, and alphabetised your CD collection, don't put it off any longer. If you really do want to shut up that tedious inner critic once and for all, you need to look your enemy straight in the face. You won't get rid of your thoughts and emotions by pushing them out of mind.

TALKING BACK TO YOUR INNER CRITIC

Here's where you learn to heckle your self-critical thinking and propose a more balanced view. If you've already begun to spot self-critical thoughts, well done – you've taken the first important step towards living life without them. Now you've identified them, it's time to question them in the same way that you questioned your anxious predictions. Remember, your self-critical thoughts are not statements of the truth about yourself, so it's time to stop acting as if they were. You need to start compiling a stock of positive, helpful and balanced alternatives to replace your critical voice.

The last two columns of your **Inner critic worksheet** are space to record these alternatives, and to assess their impact on what you originally thought and felt. The last column is a space to write down a plan of action to test out how helpful these Shiny New Thoughts are.

Here's what to fill in:

6 Shiny new thoughts

To help you come up with meaningful alternatives to your self-critical thoughts, read on to the end of the chapter, especially the five 'power questions' (pages 108–9). You'll need to rate each alternative according to how much you believe it, just as you rated the original self-critical thoughts 0 to10. Give 10 if you believe the alternative completely, 0 if you don't believe it at all, 5 if you have some belief in it. If you find you've given all of your alternatives a very low believability rating, you'll need to work through the questions again to come up with more believable ones.

7 What's your EBA?

E is for Emotions – now that you've found alternatives to your self-critical thoughts, how do you feel? Rate each feeling from 0 to 10 for intensity (10 being strongest). You should find that the intensity of your original painful emotions, recorded in the column 'How I felt', has eased off. **B is for Believability** – how far do you now believe the self-critical thoughts? Rate each one from 0 to 10, with 10 being most strongly believed. You should find that your belief in your self-critical thoughts has got weaker. **A is for Action** – what can you do? It's time to experiment again! If your heart sinks, remind yourself that this is how you will make the most powerful changes to your life – not just sitting comfortably in your armchair diligently working through this book, but getting out there, taking risks, and pushing your boundaries. Work out some experiments to test how valid your new perspectives are in real life.

TOP TIPS FOR MAKING THIS WORK

- **Don't rush it.** Some people find that questioning their self-critical thoughts and searching for alternative perspectives is easier than they thought. But don't worry too much if you find the opposite – that you can't think of anything but the same old put-downs. Self-critical thinking can become a deeply entrenched habit. Or the alternatives that you do come up may not feel believable, or seem to make a difference to your self-image. All habits take time to break – it's like taking up a new kind of exercise, except you're trying to flex mental muscles that you don't normally use. It may feel awkward and uncomfortable at first. But with practice, these muscles will grow strong and flexible. The reward for your hard work is that you will start to effortlessly nip self-critical thoughts in the bud before they get a chance to affect your feelings or the way you act. Try to fill out a sheet with one or two examples every day when you get started. Later, you won't need to write everything down, but the worksheet is useful back-up support when you need it. If you find yourself feeling stressed or unhappy, and your self-critical voice is making a come-back, go back and fill out the sheet again for as long as it takes you to regain your balance.

- **Be kind to yourself.** If something happens that upsets you, you'll probably find it difficult to be objective about your self-critical thoughts. When this happens, be gentle with yourself – your reaction is understandable and natural, but it's easy to fall into the trap of criticising yourself for not being able to cope. You can still learn from the situation by making a note of what happened to upset you, but leave off the quest for shiny new thoughts until you've settled on the situation and it's feeling less raw.

- **Good enough is *better* than perfection!** Many people with low self-confidence are actually perfectionists who set themselves sky-high standards in everything they do. For them, it's never enough to be 'good enough'. If you catch yourself falling into the perfectionist trap, remind yourself of the purpose of this whole exercise. Essentially, your ultimate aim is to increase your self-awareness. To do that, you need to learn to become a more flexible thinker. Perfectionism makes flexibility virtually impossible, and it does a good job of stifling creative thinking as well. You don't have to find the 'right' answer or put down what you think you 'should' write, just an answer that works for you – it makes sense, and seems to have a positive effect on your feelings.

- **Give yourself a break.** Beware of being hard on yourself when you find the going tough – don't pile on the criticism if you catch yourself falling back into self-critical habits. Changing how you think isn't easy and it takes time and practice. Don't expect your belief in your old thoughts and painful feelings to fade away overnight, especially if they reflect a self-image that may have been in place for many years. Self-critical thinking is like your threadbare old coat – it may look a sight, but it feels familiar. A new perspective can feel like a new coat – it looks great but it feels unfamiliar and you're not sure it's really 'you'. Once you've worn it for a while, it seems to fit you better and you can tell it's a big improvement.

THE FIVE 'POWER QUESTIONS' TO HELP YOU FIND ALTERNATIVES

Coming up with alternatives to self-critical thoughts isn't easy. These five crucial questions will help unearth even the most insidious inner critic, spotlighting its favourite put-downs and the wordless images it conjures up to make you feel awful. Remember, you already have some experience of questioning and testing your thoughts under your belt, from the work you did on checking out anxious predictions.

As you work through them, you may find that one particular question is especially revealing. (It might be Q3: *What effect does it have, thinking the way I do about myself? Do my self-critical thoughts help me, or are they just getting in the way?*) This is a powerful resource for you, so use it. Write it down on a card, stick it to your computer or fridge, or carry it in your wallet. When you're faced with a critical thought, use your 'power question' to challenge that thought.

Each question has some sub-questions to help direct your thoughts. Read through the list first, then we'll look at each in a little detail to clarify them further.

Five 'Power Questions'

Question 1: What's the evidence?

- *Am I assuming my thoughts are facts?*
- *Is there anything that suggests these thoughts are accurate?*
- *Is there anything that suggests these thoughts aren't accurate?*

Question 2: What alternatives are there?

- *Am I blinkered to other possibilities?*
- *What would an outsider say about me?*
- *What would a friend say?*

Question 3: What effect does it have, thinking the way I do about myself?

- *Do my self-critical thoughts help me, or are they just getting in the way?*
- *What point of view might be more helpful to me?*

Question 4: Where am I going wrong in the way I think about myself?

- *Do I jump to conclusions?*
- *Would I think the same about someone else?*
- *Am I using black-and-white thinking?*
- *Am I completely writing myself off as a person whenever one thing goes wrong?*
- *Am I focusing on my weaknesses and overlooking my strengths?*
- *Do I blame myself, when something isn't really my fault?*
- *Am I trying to be perfect?*

Question 5: What can I do about this?

- *How can I be more compassionate to myself?*
- *What can I do to change the situation, or to change my own thinking about it in future?*
- *Can I try acting in a less self-defeating way?*

Q 1: What's the evidence?

Am I assuming my thoughts are facts? You may not be right. Think about some of the things you used to believe, and have since realised aren't true or accurate.

Is there anything that suggests these thoughts are accurate? What actual evidence is there to support a negative view of yourself? What real facts or observations (rather than anyone's ideas or opinions) prove you are right to criticise yourself?

Is there anything that suggests these thoughts aren't accurate? What evidence, from your past or from other areas in your life, would contradict your self-critical thoughts? For example, if you're calling yourself 'stupid', what evidence is there that you're not stupid but – on the contrary – are pretty bright? Think of all your achievements.

Q 2: What alternatives are there?

Am I blinkered to other possibilities? The same situation can be viewed from different angles. How would you see this particular situation on a day when you were feeling more confident? How will it look in ten years' time? What would you say to a friend who had this problem?

What would an outsider say about me? Make sure you use some objective evidence when you think about someone else's view of you – if you come up with an alternative perspective that has no basis in reality, it won't help.

Q 3: What effect does it have, thinking the way I do about myself?

Do my self-critical thoughts help me, or are they just getting in the way? What do you want out of life? What are your goals or objectives? What do you want out of this situation? Is your self-critical thinking helping you get what you want?

What point of view might be more helpful to me? Would it help you achieve more in life, and generally feel better, if you thought about yourself in a more encouraging way – more balanced and more compassionate?

Q 4: Where am I going wrong in the way I think about myself?

Do I jump to conclusions? Do you decide on the facts without proper evidence to support your point of view – decide your boss didn't smile at you in the lift because he's not happy with your work? You have no idea what's behind his behaviour – he may look unhappy because he has a headache! If you have low self-confidence, you're probably in the habit of jumping to whatever conclusion reflects badly on you. Review the evidence, look for facts, think 'bigger picture'.

Would I think the same about someone else? Are you applying double standards? Are you much harder on yourself than anyone else? Are the standards you apply to yourself much higher and more rigid than you expect from other people? Ask yourself how you would react if someone you cared about had a similar problem. Would you say they were 'weak' or 'pathetic', and that they should know better? Or would you sympathise with them and give them some encouragement to help them get the situation into perspective and look for ways of dealing with it?

Am I using black-and-white thinking? 'Black-and-white' thinking oversimplifies matters into one view or the opposite. People aren't usually completely good or bad, stupid or smart, weak or strong, but a mixture of the two. Things that happen aren't normally total disasters or total successes, but somewhere between. Do you tend to think in extremes? Check for words such as *always/never, everyone/no one, everything/nothing*.

Am I completely writing myself off as a person whenever one thing goes wrong? Do you dismiss your whole worth as a person on the basis of one thing you did or said? Somebody doesn't seem to like you, so there must be something wrong with you? You made one mistake at work, so you're a complete failure? Judging your whole self on the basis of one situation simply doesn't make sense. If there's something you excel at, does that make you a totally wonderful person? No, that would be nonsense, and it's the same for things that don't go well for you. Remember, you're most likely to fall into a self-critical pattern of thinking when you feel low, because you'll be screening out positives and giving all your attention to the negatives.

Am I focusing on my weaknesses and overlooking my strengths? Are you concentrating on things you don't seem to be good at, and screening out your strengths and talents? When your mind ruminates, does it remember all the times you've made mistakes, been rejected, or felt you've failed? When you're feeling really low, it may be difficult to credit yourself with even one good quality or talent. Of course there are things you're not very good at, things you've done that you regret, and aspects of yourself that you would prefer to change. That's true for everyone. But what about the *other* side of the coin – the things you're good at? What do other people appreciate about you? What do you like about yourself? How have you coped with difficulties and stresses in your life? What are your personal strengths and good qualities?

Q 5: What can I do about this?

How can I be more compassionate to myself? How could you test whether a new, kinder perspective is an improvement on your inner critic? Could you make a conscious effort to be compassionate towards yourself for a day, and see how it feels?

What can I do to change the situation, or to change my own thinking about it in future? Do you need to distance yourself from a friend who always makes you feel bad about yourself? Do you need to find another job that is better suited to your true passion and talents? Or do you simply need to change the way you think (e.g. stop jumping to conclusions, stop blaming yourself)?

Can I try acting in a less self-defeating way? You've done the thinking, now it's time for action. Could you test out your new ways of thinking, in the same way you tested out your anxious predictions – by trying them out in real life? Remember, when it comes to change, there's no substitute for experience. Sometimes actions speak louder than words.

➤ *FIND OUT MORE ABOUT THIS:* Turn to Chapter 6 to learn about self-acceptance.

If you tend to focus on the bad and ignore the good, your inner critic is acting like an inner *prosecutor*, alert for every flaw and weakness and always ready to condemn. You need to develop an equally strong inner *defender* who will present the evidence for the defence. And when you're in the dock, most importantly you need an inner judge and jury who will base their view on *all* the evidence, rather than condemning you solely on the basis of evidence presented by one side.

Do I blame myself, when something isn't really my fault? When things go wrong, do you consider all the possible reasons for that, or do you tend to assume immediately that it must be your fault? If a friend doesn't return your last two text messages, for example, do you tend to assume it's because you've done something to annoy them?

There are all sorts of reasons for things seeming to go wrong. Sometimes, it may be connected to something you've said or done. But often, other factors need to be taken into account. Your friend may simply be busy, or he may not realise you're expecting answers to your texts, or he may even be having a family crisis. He may be intending to call you at the weekend when he's got more time to talk. If you automatically assume responsibility for something that's gone wrong, you're ignoring other possibilities. What other possible reasons can you think of? If you keep an open mind about whose 'fault' it is, you may discover you are less to blame than you thought – or indeed that what happened had nothing to do with you.

Am I trying to be perfect? Do you expect to be able to cope fine with everything life throws at you? Do you believe everything should be done to the highest standard, in all circumstances and regardless of the cost to yourself? It's just not realistic to expect perfection all the time – you're setting yourself up to fail. Accepting you can't always achieve 100 per cent doesn't mean you permanently lower your standards, but it does mean you can set yourself realistic targets and give yourself credit when you reach them. Then you can learn from your mistakes, and feel motivated to keep going and try again. As Sir Winston Churchill said, success is the ability to go from one failure to the next with no loss of enthusiasm!

FAKE IT TILL YOU MAKE IT!

Your habits have a powerful effect on your thoughts and your emotions. Up to now, the habitual way you've been thinking about yourself, and treating yourself, follows patterns that keep your self-confidence low. Here are some ideas for establishing a new pattern – the habit of healthy self-confidence. Willingness to experiment is the key. You may feel a bit awkward and artificial to start with – after all, you're strengthening your mental 'muscles'. But as the saying goes, fake it until you make it! If you do these things regularly, you'll find that after a while they become second nature.

- **Accept compliments graciously.** When someone tells you they like your shirt, don't say, 'Oh, it's ancient.' Smile and say, 'Thank you.' When someone praises a dish you've prepared, don't tell them it was a bit overcooked – smile and say 'Thank you!'

- **Stop automatic apologising.** If someone knocks into you at the supermarket, do you say sorry? When a waiter brings you the wrong meal, do you say, 'I'm sorry, but this isn't what I ordered'? Notice how many times you say 'sorry' in one day and start by reducing them by half. Try to think of what you really mean to say, and a more effective way of phrasing it: 'Excuse me, this isn't what I ordered. I asked for the …'

- **Say no before you say yes.** When someone asks you to do something that will involve you committing time and energy that you're not sure you have, say, 'I'm not sure about that, I'll have to check my diary and get back to you.' Only say yes immediately if you know you'll have the time and want to do it.

Anna's Inner critic worksheet

Day/ Date/ Time	What is happening	How I feel: emotions & sensations *(Rate each, 0 to10)*	What I'm thinking *(Rate belief in each thought, 0 to 10)*	Knee-jerk reactions	My shiny new thoughts! Use the five 'power questions' to find other perspectives on your thoughts. *(Rate belief in each new perspective, 0 to 10)*	EBA a) Emotions How I feel, with my shiny new thoughts. *(Rate each feeling, 0 to10 for intensity)* b) Believability How much I now believe my self-critical thoughts. *(Rate each thought for believability, 0 to10)* c) Actions What can I do? Experiments!
Wed. 25th June 6.45 pm	New boyfriend hasn't called for two days	Anxiety 6 Low mood 8 Hopeless 5 Headache 3	Here we go again, another man who doesn't want to know me 10 I'm so hopeless at relationships, no one wants to be with me 7	Can't stop checking my phone every five minutes in case I've missed a text Felt very distracted at work and didn't get a lot done	He's intending to call but has been busy at work 4 He's wondering why I haven't called him 3 He doesn't want to see me again, but it's for personal reasons, not any fault of mine 5	a) Anxiety 3 Low mood 2 Hopeless 3 b) 5/5/3 c) Send him a friendly but casual email, suggesting meeting up again If he doesn't reply, assume he's not interested and move on

ESSENTIAL NOTE: HOME MESSAGES FROM THIS CHAPTER

I must have done something to put him off 9

- **Watch your language.** Your brain believes what you most often say. If you tell people often enough that your job is a 'nightmare', or that you are 'so fat', or 'hopelessly disorganised', or that you have 'an appalling memory', you'll start to believe it! Self-deprecating humour is an easy habit to get into but it can escalate and have a direct effect on your self-image. When someone asks you how you are, or how your work is going, could you think of something truthfully positive – or even neutral – to say instead of automatically putting yourself down?

ESSENTIAL TAKE-HOME MESSAGES FROM THIS CHAPTER

- **Knowledge is power.** Your inner critic is your enemy and, to defeat it, you need to know how it operates. It's not easy to focus on that self-critical running commentary in your mind, but ignoring it won't make it go away. You need to challenge it, come up with believable alternatives, and test them out.

- **Window shopping isn't enough!** A new jacket may look just your style on the hanger, but until you try it on you don't really know whether it will suit you. Theory only goes so far – you need to try on your 'shiny new thoughts' for size and see if they fit, and whether they make positive changes to the way you feel and act.

- **Compassion has power.** You thrive on encouragement, not criticism! If you secretly fear that if you ease up on yourself you'll never achieve anything in life, think about this: Would you teach someone how to do something new by criticising them and telling them they're bound to fail, every time they made a mistake? If not, why do you think you'll get results by treating yourself that way?

Life Lesson

Mental notes don't have half the power of written records. So if you really want to make changes, keep writing.

6

ACCEPTING YOURSELF FOR WHO YOU ARE

There's still a taboo against positive thinking in many societies, cultures and families. 'Being full of it', 'a big-head', 'conceited' or 'arrogant' are criticisms aimed at people who appear to be over-confident, or proud of their abilities or achievements. 'They're heading for a fall,' might be the next comment and we're almost hoping that they get knocked back. In Australia, it's known as 'tall poppy syndrome' – stand too tall, and you'll get cut down. In Britain, the tabloids love nothing better than a fallen idol, and it seems almost inevitable that today's hottest star will be lambasted for their behaviour, career choices or appearance further down the line – 'they'll get their comeuppance'.

So it's no surprise that many of us find feeling good about ourselves doesn't come easy. Thinking well of yourself, and allowing yourself to acknowledge your good points, can feel very uncomfortable – it may feel too much like boasting, to you. Parents worry they will 'spoil' a child by giving it too much praise. At school, academically gifted children may be bullied or ostracised and play down their talents as a result. The message is that people who feel good about themselves aren't acceptable, so we learn to put ourselves down or, to use an old saying, 'hide our light under a bushel'.

Self-acceptance, and learning to feel good about yourself, can feel frightening – you may worry that losing your self-doubt will make people reject you for being 'full of yourself'. But the aim of this book isn't to take you to the other end of the spectrum from where you are now, thinking you're the best thing since sliced bread, so perfect that everything you do or say is right! It's about finding balance and living *authentically* – living in a way that reflects who you truly are. It's about accepting the good as well as the negative points about yourself, just as you accept them in other people. In fact, the more accepting you are of yourself, the more accepting you will be of other people, so your ability to form close relationships, and truly love and be loved by other people, will grow stronger.

Like self-criticism, ignoring or undervaluing positive aspects of yourself has been holding you back from achieving your true potential. Ask yourself, do you *really* think that self-acceptance leads to complacency? That if you embrace your strengths and talents, and accept that you deserve the good things in life, you'll feel so smug and self-satisfied that you'll never achieve anything else as long as you live? Self-acceptance is a realistic appraisal of your individuality, and it's an important aspect of self-confidence. One reason your self-confidence has never reached its natural potential is because you've refused to fully embrace your unique talents or abilities.

This book isn't a series of mind-tricks designed to convince you you're amazing, whatever you've done in your life. It's the opposite of that. Your goal is reality: accepting yourself for who you really are, giving you an honest, realistic, accurate and kindly point of view.

In this chapter, you will learn . . .

- How to bring your positive qualities into the spotlight, and take the first step towards accepting the good things about yourself.
- A simple, easy way to bring your good points into focus every day.
- How recognising and valuing your good points has an immediate impact on how you feel about yourself and how you go about your daily life.
- Why daily pleasures are not a luxury, but essential for your mental health and well-being.
- How tackling your 'to-do' list will boost your self-confidence.

🖉 *TIME TO GET WRITING:*

Explore your individual talents

According to the psychologist Martin Seligman, the key to finding lasting inner contentment is discovering your 'signature strengths' (such as optimism, diligence, integrity, playfulness, generosity) and then trying to live a life that makes the most of them. This next exercise will help you work out your own 'signature strengths' – the combination of qualities, skills, interests and passions that's unique to you. This is a great way of reinforcing a more positive view of yourself. As a bonus, it should be a wake-up call, alerting you to the extent to which you ignore or discount the positives about yourself. By the time you've finished this exercise, you should be more alert to these disclaimers, and better able to see them adjust old thinking habits, instead of taking them seriously. Dismissing your good points is a habit which will weaken, so long as you keep your mental disclaimers in perspective and learn to put them to one side so they don't stop you thinking from a more positive perspective.

What to do

You're going to make a list of your positive qualities. Answering some helpful questions will get you going. If your doubts about yourself are already starting to ease off, or they only tend to surface in particularly challenging situations, you may find this quite easy. Not everyone who lacks self-confidence is completely unaware of their good points. But if your Bottom Line is well entrenched, you may find listing positive qualities a near impossible task. Do you find that you could easily list your weaknesses and bad points, but when asked to come up with something positive your mind literally goes blank? That's not unusual in people who have been discouraged from thinking well of themselves while they were growing up. If your achievements have never been acknowledged (never mind celebrated), and you've picked up the message that your needs are unimportant or invisible, then appreciating yourself is going to feel alien. But this doesn't mean you'll always think this way – with time, you will be able to see good things about yourself and value them. Investing time in this exercise is the first step. If you really can't get started, it may help to get a close friend or family member that you can trust to help you come up with a first-draft list.

What you need

A sheet of paper, a pencil, a quiet place where you won't be interrupted, and plenty of time. Make sure you have somewhere comfortable to sit and try to feel relaxed before you start, maybe by playing your favourite music in the background or just sitting quietly for a few moments, slowing down your breathing and focusing your attention on the breath.

How to do it

Make a list of as many of the good things about yourself as you can think of. Don't worry if it feels hard at first, or you quickly write down a few then find your mind goes blank. Remember, you're trying to think from a new perspective and make new 'pathways' in your brain which will take time to establish. Then, when you've come up with as many qualities as you can, put your list somewhere safe, but keep it in the back of your mind. When new ideas come to you, add them to your list.

Coaching questions

If you're struggling with this exercise, it doesn't mean you don't have many good qualities – you've just spent a long time filtering them out and focusing on the negative. The following questions can help to shift that negative filter and focus on what's positive about you. Here is the list of questions – more detail on each of them follows.

- What do you like about yourself, however minor?
- What positive qualities do you possess?
- What have you achieved in your life, however small?

- What challenges have you faced?
- What gifts or talents do you have (even small ones)?
- What skills have you gained?
- What do other people like or value in you?
- What qualities and actions, that you value in others, do you have as well?
- What bad things don't apply to you?
- How would your best friend describe you?

What do you like about yourself, however minor? Scan your memory for any stored scenes where your background emotion was one of self-appreciation – even if it was only there for a micro-second. Did it cross your mind that you may be blessed with patience the last time you visited your elderly aunt? Do you feel good after you've taken the time to really talk to your children? Do you have a secret suspicion that you're actually a good mechanic or a creative cook? Do you stay calm in a crisis, or come up with great solutions to problems?

What positive qualities do you possess? It doesn't matter if you don't show these qualities all the time – even the funniest comedians don't crack jokes 24/7! And even the most tolerant people find their patience runs out at times. Everyone has off-days. If you can recognise a quality in yourself, you need to give yourself the credit for it, whether or not it lives up to your 'perfect' ideal. Don't discount a good quality just because it's not perfect.

What have you achieved in your life, however small? It doesn't have to be Nobel-prize material. It could be learning to upload photos onto your PC and sending them to friends and family, or competing in a local 5k charity race, or being able to knock up a delicious spaghetti bolognese.

What challenges have you faced? Are you dismissing the fact that you've overcome some considerable challenges, problems or anxieties? Do you ever look back and wonder how on earth you did it? So what does this say about you – does it suggest you have courage, persistence, tenacity? Being proactive enough to pick up this book is another sign of your courage – take some credit it for it.

What gifts or talents do you have (even small ones)? There's more to talent than making it to the Olympics. Small things count – even if you're not perfect at something. Can you put people at their ease, put together a flat-pack without swearing, transform an outfit with the right accessories, or do a fantastic karaoke rendition of 'My Way'? These are your gifts – when are you going to stop ignoring them?

What skills have you gained? Think about all the different areas of your life and note down skills you have in all of them, however basic. Can you play tennis or do front crawl? Can you work PowerPoint or Excel? Can you make a sponge cake that rises every time? Can you order lunch in another language? Can you coax even the most wilted of plants and shrubs back to life? Include work skills, domestic skills, people skills, academic skills, sporting skills, and leisure skills – they all count.

What do other people like or value in you? You probably get regular feedback from people about what you're doing well that you don't take much notice of. Now it's time to pay attention to it. What do friends ask your advice about, or ask you to do for them? What do they compliment you on? What do they rave about?

What qualities and actions, that you value in others, do you have as well? You'd be likely to find this exercise a lot easier if you were turning the spotlight on someone else's good points rather than your own. But sometimes another person's good qualities can mirror your own. Are there any positive character traits in people that have a familiar feel to them? Perhaps you've acted in a similar way in the past. It doesn't matter if you feel the other person does it better than you – simply acknowledge that you share the quality, even if only to a limited extent. Or are there aspects of yourself that you would appreciate if you found them in another person? Are you a good listener? Do you take care not to let your personal problems affect your mood at work? Do you often lend people books or CDs you think they'll enjoy? Write down anything that you'd find appealing if it was done by someone else.

What bad things don't apply to you? Sometimes it becomes easier to think of positive qualities if you start by thinking of negative qualities. It may sound perverse, but try it and you may unearth good points you'd previously overlooked! It's also strangely good fun. So give your imagination free rein to think of some bad qualities (e.g. judgemental, untrustworthy, dishonest, cowardly, fickle, manipulative). Do any of these apply to you? If not, then consider the possibility that you're the opposite (open-minded, trustworthy, honest, brave, consistent, fair-minded). Write down these qualities, even if you feel you're not 'perfect' at them, or you don't act like this all the time.

How would your best friend describe you? Think about your closest friend, or a trusted work colleague or family member. How would they describe you? Would you feel comfortable asking them? If so, it might be easier to do by email. Is there someone close to you, who you respect, and that you could ask to email a list of the things that they appreciate about you? (It goes without saying that you shouldn't ask anyone who you even remotely suspect is a 'toxic' friend, or a family member who on the whole causes you more grief than happiness.) You may find it too cringe-worthy, but if there is someone you trust who really cares about you, asking them to do this for you can be a revelation. They can list qualities you would never have thought of and it can bring you closer and strengthen your relationship. To say thank you, you could offer to write a list for them in return.

Making your list work for you

Listing your positive qualities is an important first step and hopefully it's made you feel good, too. But that feel-good buzz will soon wear off if you never look at your list again. You need to use it! Your list is a good starting point for an important awareness-raising exercise. The aim is to retune your mental antenna so it picks up evidence of your good points in action. You'll need to make a conscious effort to do this at first, but ultimately it should become your 'default' mode of thinking, so awareness of your good points is always with you to lift your spirits. When you get to that stage you won't have to make a special effort to notice the good things you do or when things go well – your mind will do it automatically. But for this mental retuning to happen, you will need to find a way of putting your good points in the spotlight.

How to do it

Take a few days to think about your list and add as many items as you can. Then choose a time when you can be undisturbed, and feel comfortable and relaxed. Start by reading the list slowly to yourself, pausing and trying to immerse yourself in each word. Let the ideas sink in. When you've carefully read from top to bottom, start again at the top. This time, as you consider each item, bring to mind a particular situation that gave you evidence of that good quality or talent or achievement. Take the time to recall the memory as vividly as you can. Close your eyes, and remember where you were, who you were with, what you could see, hear and smell, how you felt, what exactly you did and what the consequences were.

Kevin, for example, who you met in chapter 2, had 'being a good friend' on his list. He thought hard and remembered going for a drink with a few workmates after work. Kevin had noticed that one of his colleagues, Ali, seemed subdued. As they were walking home in the same direction, Ali had confided that he'd had an argument with his wife and was feeling really low. Kevin let Ali talk about it, offering encouraging words to show he was listening, but didn't attempt to jump in with any advice or with his opinion or his own similar experiences. He had a feeling that Ali just needed to get it all off his chest. The next day, Kevin stepped in to take on a task the boss was planning to give Ali, and his mate looked grateful. Kevin accepted this as an example of his own sensitivity and emotional intelligence.

The more fully you can immerse yourself in this exercise, the more powerful it is. And what's great about it is that as well as the long-term effect, it's also an instant mood-booster. Take a moment to sit with your feelings. Can you feel your self-confidence growing a little stronger? Is there a blossoming sense of self-acceptance that wasn't there before? And doesn't it feel great?

What if this doesn't happen?

Then maybe your inner critic has crept in under the radar and is filling your subconscious with subtle disqualifiers. 'Creative? You? That's a joke!' 'Ethical-minded? In your dreams, maybe!' Is your critic coming up with a put-down as quickly as you come up with a good quality – telling you it was nothing, anyone can be like that and in fact loads of people do it better than you? Or is it just telling you that you should be ashamed of being so smug? Or maybe it's just pointing out that OK, you may be compassionate, supportive or whatever from time to time but it doesn't count because you're not always like that. Or is it devaluing your qualities by telling you they're pretty ordinary ('Who *isn't* a good listener?').

When these put-downs intrude, can you notice their presence without getting tangled up in them? Think, 'Oh there you are, "Voice", I wondered when you'd turn up! Thanks for your input but I only need positive comments right now.' If the critical voice won't shut up, then you may need to revise Chapter 5, and perhaps fill in another **Inner critic worksheet**.

If you go through your list regularly, and immerse yourself in your positive memories, you'll be able to bring them to mind in detail when you need to. You can also make the most of the following instant mood-enhancer: it's a simple trick recommended by practitioners of NLP (neuro-linguistic programming) such as Paul McKenna. If you're about to go into a challenging meeting at work, spend ten minutes beforehand quietly recalling past meetings that have gone well, or immersing yourself in memories that highlight your talents or skills at work, and you'll walk into the room feeling more confident, open, relaxed and ready to think creatively and effectively.

YOUR POSITIVES NOTEBOOK

Now you've got your list of positive qualities and you've spent time bringing each one to life so that it feels real and believable, you need a way of keeping this awareness 'real'. This is where a Positives Notebook comes in.

✎ TIME TO GET WRITING:

Thinking about your good points

Buy yourself a new pocket-size notebook with an attractive cover. Don't use a notebook you've already written in – buying a special one will help to mark this in your mind as a project that's worth taking seriously.

Write down examples of how you use your good points, skills or qualities in everyday life, preferably as they occur. Your objective is to reach the point where you automatically notice good things that you do, by putting them in your mental spotlight. Aim to record three examples every day. If you find that keeping your Positives Notebook with you doesn't work, take time at the end of each day, before you go to bed, to write down your three things. (If you find you have more than three, do write them all down, but try to aim for at least three every day.) If you can't think of anything, read through your list of positive qualities to try to get in the right frame of mind. For each entry, write down what you did and then sum up the quality, skill, strength or talent that it illustrates. Charlotte's example will give you the idea.

From Charlotte's 'Positives Notebook'

Tuesday 20th March

1   Spent an extra hour after work researching colours for the new design. (diligent, passionate about design)

2   Remembered it was Jane's birthday on Saturday and found the perfect card to send her. (thoughtful, good friend)

3   Cycled to work and back to get some exercise and save money. (motivated, adventurous)

At the end of the week, review each page and let the experiences really sink in. Recreate each one in your mind's eye – almost as if you were reliving it. Make the memory as vivid as you can, and see if you can call up the feeling you experienced. After a few weeks, you'll have created an invaluable source of confidence-boosting memories that you can re-run whenever you're feeling stressed, low or bad about yourself, or you just generally need a lift. Every day, you will be honing your awareness of your positive qualities in action. In time, noticing them will become a habit – part of a new way of appreciating yourself.

THE POWER OF PLEASURE

By now, you've put your good points firmly in the spotlight, and allowed them to take centre stage in your mind, helping to squeeze out the dark shadows of self-criticism and negative predictions. You're beginning to accept that you are a worthwhile person. Now it's time to look at how often you reward yourself for all the effort you put into your life, and the good you do. Making sure that you do one thing every day that brings you true pleasure is not a luxury, or an indulgence – it's essential for your mental health. We're not talking about 'me time', a phrase that's become so overused that it's almost meaningless. It's not about being self-indulgent, and doesn't have to involve lying in a bubble bath by candlelight (unless you really want to!). It's about taking responsibility for your own happiness and enhancing your self-confidence by giving yourself credit for your everyday achievements, however small. Don't underestimate how important this is in your quest to change your self-image. It's true that increasing the pleasure in your life and focusing on your good points lifts your mood. But this is not just about feeling good – when your mood is lifted, it's also easier to fight self-criticism and stop the vicious circle that keeps your self-confidence low.

✍ TIME TO GET WRITING:

Starting a Daily Activity Diary (DAD)

Happiness is smaller than you think. Small pleasures and tiny achievements have a big impact. But it's amazing how many of us spend the majority of our days, every day, doing things we feel we 'should' do, rather than things we actually enjoy or that we feel have a point to them. What about you? This exercise will show you clearly how you spend your time – and how much of it is making you happy, or unhappy. You're going to keep a diary to help you to identify days when there are little or no activities that bring you pleasure, so you can think about changes you could make to bring a positive experience into your life every day.

How to do it

You need to fill in a timetable of your life for at least a week, detailing what you do during each hour of the day. Choose an 'average' week, not a special one such as when you're on holiday. As well as noting down what you do in every hour, you'll also write down what you get from it (you'll find out how to do that in the next section). You can see the idea from two days in Charlotte's daily activity diary.

The benefit of an hour-by-hour record is that it prompts you to notice what is going on in real detail. At the end of the day, you have an accurate record with lots of information, rather than a vague impression of how things have gone. So, for each hour:

1 Write down what you did. Simply make a note of how you filled each time-slot. But try to be specific. Activity doesn't just mean being active. Sitting with a cup of tea, planning the week in your head, or worrying about a problem, pottering around, getting ready for tomorrow or trying to find something you've lost, or sitting on the sofa flicking through TV channels, even sleeping – these are all activities. The more specific your entries, the more useful the exercise.

2 Give it a 'pleasure' rating. Think about how much you enjoyed what you did. Then rate it between 0 and 10, with P10 being the biggest enjoyment, P5 being moderate enjoyment, and P0 being no enjoyment at all. You may be surprised at just how much variation there is in your pleasure level, depending on what you do. Rating your activities this way can be very revealing and show you what you *actually* enjoy doing, as opposed to what you think you *should* enjoy! And you may realise that some things aren't as pleasurable as you thought (seeing certain friends, for example). In her Daily Activity Diary, Charlotte gave 'Cycling to work' a P6 as she enjoyed being in the fresh air and getting exercise, but didn't enjoy a section of the route that went through heavy traffic. She gave herself a P10 for the meal she enjoyed with friends – the food was delicious, everyone was in a relaxed and upbeat mood, and conversation flowed easily. But she gave a P2 rating to the drink that followed afterwards – she was tired, the bar was crowded, they couldn't find anywhere to sit, and the music was so loud they couldn't talk.

3 Give it an 'achievement' rating. This refers to how much each activity felt like an achievement – it's your mental pat on the back, your 'Good for you!' A10 would mean a big achievement – Charlotte gave herself an A9 for lunch with her manager as she made an effort to highlight her achievements and talk about what was going well and also where she felt she needed more support, rather than adopting her old approach, which was to put herself down. She had to push herself and it wasn't easy, but she did it, so she gave herself a high 'A' rating. A5 would mean a moderate achievement. Charlotte gave herself A5 for taking a quick walk on Friday afternoon – she knew it would make her work more productive and help clear her head, but she had to overcome 'guilt' feelings at leaving the office during work hours. She gave herself an A7 rating for having muesli for breakfast – she usually skips breakfast altogether but she's making an effort to fit it in, and managed it that day even though she was pushed for time. Give yourself an A0 rating if there was zero effort involved – Charlotte gave herself A0 for an evening at home watching reality TV shows.

Charlotte's Daily Activity Diary

TIME/ DAY	Th	Fr
6-7	Sleep P10/A0	Sleep P10/A0
7-8	Got up/shower/got dressed/ate healthy muesli P5/A7	Got up/shower/got dressed/ate healthy muesli P5/A7
8-9	Cycled to work P6/A10	Raining, caught crowded bus to work P1/A0
9-10	Worked on new designs P6/A8	Team meeting P2/A6
10-11	Ditto	Ditto
11-12	Talking to office assistant about a work problem P3/A7	Admin catch-up P2/A7
12-1	Worked on new designs P5/A3	Ditto
1-2	Shopping for new T-shirt P9/A2	Lunch with manger P2/A9
2-3	Meeting with new client P4/A8	Ditto
3-4	Ditto	Calling phone company to query huge mobile phone bill P0/A10 Quick walk to get fresh air P9/A5 Working on new design P8/A8

Time		
4–5	Chatting to work colleagues P8/A6	Worked on new design P8/A8
5–6	Writing up meeting notes and client objectives/ catching up with emails P2/A8	Ditto
6–7	Cycled home P4/A10	Office drinks for birthday P5/A8
7–8	Feeding cat, cooking stir-fry, eating, drinking glass of wine P8/A0	Met friends for Thai meal P10/A0
8–9	Talking on phone to mum P3/A7	Ditto
9–10	Watching reality TV P7/A0	Ditto
10–11	Reading new novel in bed P9/A1	Drink in crowded bar P2/A2
11–12	Sleep P9/A0	Getting home on late-night bus P0/A9
12–1	Ditto	Sleep P10/A0

Bear in mind that 'achievement' doesn't only refer to major events like running a marathon, spring-cleaning the house from top to bottom or organising a fundraising event for charity. Every achievement is relative, after all – a big thing for you might be a 'piece of cake' for someone else, and vice versa. And don't forget that something that you do regularly can feel like more – or less – of an achievement depending on your state of mind. When you're feeling emotionally vulnerable, or you're tired, stressed or feel unwell, even relatively routine activities (being patient with the children, going for a short walk, preparing a healthy meal) can be big achievements.

So for each activity, think about how you felt at the time, and take it into account when you give it a rating. Your pre-breakfast walk, which you would normally rate around A5, might deserve an A8 or A9 on a cold, rainy morning or when you wake up feeling tired and unmotivated. So you're really rating each achievement *according to how you felt at the time*. Giving yourself credit for these minor triumphs over adversity plays an important role in building up self-confidence.

You'll probably find that some activities are mainly A activities, and some are mainly P, but that others are a mix of the two. Going to an exercise class might deserve a good A rating if you feel self-conscious about exercising or you're not sure you'll be able to keep up. But if you started to relax and enjoy once the class got underway, it might warrant a high P rating, too.

TOP TIPS FOR MAKING THIS WORK

- **Do it for at least seven days.** You need to start noticing patterns and get a clear idea of how you spend your time. One week may be enough, but some people find that they need two weeks.

- **Keep it with you.** You'll get the most out of the exercise if you update your Diary regularly throughout the day. It's amazing how many things we forget we've done in a busy day. Plus, your ratings will also be more accurate the closer you do them to the actual event. Relying on your memory isn't as effective, and especially if your thinking still tends to focus on the negative and plays down your successes – especially on days when you feel low. And if you put off recording what you do, you're more likely to find filling in the sheet a chore, and give up.

- **Review it daily.** At the end of each day, take a few minutes to reflect on what you've recorded. See what springs out at you – was it a low pleasure day or were there plenty of good P ratings? What gave you the highest sense of achievement? What gave you the lowest? Does anything surprise you? What would you do less of, or more of, based on your A and P ratings? Jot down your thoughts at the bottom of the record sheet – this is the information you're going to use to make changes in your life.

TIME TO MAKE CHANGES

Step 1: Look at what jumps out at you so far

Your DAD shows low P ratings. This is a big sign that you're either not prioritising pleasure, or that you don't really enjoy the things you do for 'fun'. When you're busy, it's so easy to think, 'I don't have time for that today, I'll do it tomorrow.' But somehow, that 'tomorrow' never comes! Women in particular tend to put themselves at the bottom of a long to-do list, and only feel they 'deserve' time for themselves when they've sorted out everyone else's needs. But carving out even a small amount of time for pleasure every day can have a big impact. Or perhaps you do have time for leisure, but aren't really enjoying the things you do with it. Have you got into a routine that's become a bit stale? Do you need to try a new hobby, or just do something different?

It may also be your thoughts rather than the activities themselves that are limiting the pleasure in your life. Do you find you didn't enjoy something that should have been pleasurable because you were preoccupied with other things? Or do you find yourself making mental comparisons with how things used to be in the past? Or thinking about how things should be in your ideal life? It's hard to fully immerse yourself in an activity and really enjoy it if your mind is elsewhere. Watch out for this tendency to wander and try to refocus your mind in the 'here and now' – notice the sights and sounds around you and really listen to what people are saying. If 'killjoy' thoughts continue to demand your attention, then write them down and question them as you learned to do with anxious predictions and self-critical thoughts.

If you find nothing much brings you enjoyment in the same way as it used to, you may be suffering from depression. Go back to the checklist in chapter 1 on pages 12–13 – if five or more symptoms have lasted for at least two weeks, it would be best to talk to your GP.

Your DAD shows low A ratings. A sense of achievement is a crucial part of confidence-building. If your achievement ratings are consistently low, you either need to tweak your daily schedule to allow for more activities that give you a sense of achievement, or adjust your attitude! It may be that you rarely do anything challenging, or that allows you to use your skills, or to feel competent. This is a real possibility if your lack of self-confidence means that you worry about how well you'll do things or be able to cope. Or maybe you're waiting until you feel 'up to it' or ready to cope with something new. If so, then do some more work on your anxious and self-critical thoughts. Remember, *doing* something is the single best way to change the way you feel. Don't wait until you're motivated. Can you set yourself a small goal every day that could give you a sense of achievement?

It's also worth checking your attitude – is your inner critic disparaging the challenging activities you're already doing? Remember, it's well practised at undermining you and subtly suggesting that what you've achieved wasn't anything special, anyone could do it, and actually, you didn't do it that well anyway. That probably sounds familiar if one of your Rules for Living is to do everything perfectly. Have you set such high standards for yourself that it's virtually impossible to feel good about what you've done – your everyday small successes are just not special enough, or they're not unique ('lots of other people do the same') or they could have been done faster or more efficiently.

If your inner critic is well entrenched, you could simply be out of the habit of giving yourself credit for what you achieve from day to day. One of the great things about completing a task is basking in a sense of satisfaction at a 'job well done' – or at least feeling a warm glow of achievement. But if you never feel this when you've ticked off a task on your to-do list, and instead feel the opposite, and are left with a sense of unease, doubts about how well you've done the job, or worry about everything that's left to be done, then you may need to go back to the previous chapter and do more work on your inner critic. Don't feel you've failed – you're changing the habits of a lifetime so it's not surprising it takes time. Try putting the negative thoughts that fill your mind when you've completed a task into an **Inner critic record sheet**, and then repeat the exercises. This doesn't mean you're not doing well at working through this book – it means you're tackling old mental habits with courage and persistence. And, if you keep going, you'll get there.

Charlotte noticed that a critical voice piped up and had lots to say when she started the Daily Activity Diary, but rather than simply ignoring it, she challenged the thoughts head-on by writing them down and coming up with alternatives.

Charlotte's inner critic record sheet	
Self-critical thoughts	Alternatives
You'll never stick at this diary – I don't know why you're even trying	If I keep it with me, I'll keep on top of it. So far, I'm doing fine and there's no reason to assume that won't continue
This is sort of embarrassing. None of your friends would do this	It's something I'm doing for me, not for anyone else to look at. I'm going to learn a lot from it
So you had a healthy breakfast, would anyone think that's such a big deal if you told them?	I think it's a big deal and that's what counts. I made a resolution to eat a healthy breakfast more often and I did it even though I was running late and it would have been easy to skip it. And I noticed I had more energy all morning
I can't believe you're writing down that you watched trash TV – no wonder no one takes you seriously!	Watching TV helps me relax and switch off from work and it's irrelevant what anyone else thinks about it

Charlotte's responses show that she's getting better at acting more kindly and with more tolerance towards herself, instead of putting herself down. You'll see that her critical voice echoes her Bottom Line that she is a joke and that nothing she does is likely to be taken seriously by others. But did you think 'Hey, you go, girl!' when she answered back her critical voice? You can probably see that she's getting better at being kind to herself, and is feeling quietly pleased at her small successes. She's treating herself as someone who deserves credit, relaxation and pleasure – which is what she is, and what *you* are too.

Step 2: Making changes

Small changes can bring big results. You may already have some ideas, from reviewing your DAD, of things you'd like to add, or do more of, and things you'd like to drop or do less of. Now it's time to put those ideas into action, and do some forward planning, to make sure that any changes you do make achieve a balance that suits you between Achievement (challenges, obligations, or simple tasks) and Pleasure (enjoyment and relaxation).

Try looking for suitable slots in your DAD. Where could you make space – what could you drop, or cut down on? If you're feeling low, scheduling in changes means they're more likely to happen than simply waiting until you 'feel like it'. If exercise makes you feel better, but somehow you never get around to it, scheduling it into a specific time-slot every day may help. That's also good for perfectionists or if you find it difficult to put yourself first – sticking to your scheduled 'appointment' may feel easier than simply taking some time for yourself. Another approach is to jot down a few things you want to add into your day, then work out where to fit them in. Do you want to do more reading, or talk to long-distance friends or family more often? What could you tweak or drop from your day to fit them in?

Your aim is to make this second nature, so you automatically factor in little treats and pleasures, and tiny goals or challenges, every day, without using a written plan. But even once you've reached this stage, you might find it helpful at times to return to a written plan – when you've got a busy time coming up, or you're feeling under stress. Think of it as personal time management – you'll never get this time again, so you need to make the most of every day rather than telling yourself you'll have time for fun 'in the future' or 'when I'm not so busy!'

Cut down on screen time!

The average adult watches four hours of TV every day. Cutting that time in half frees up an extra two hours a day to devote to activities that make you feel good, or give you a sense of accomplishment. And there's an added bonus – you could also lose weight. In a study from the University of Vermont, viewers who cut their TV time in half burned an extra 119 calories a day, enough to lose a pound of fat a month.

Plan a great day!

1 Choose a good time to plan. Most people choose either first thing in the morning, or the night before, depending on what works for them. If your mornings are a hectic rush, it's probably better to do it in the evening, maybe by keeping a piece of paper by your bed and jotting down ideas before you go to sleep. But if your energy levels are at their lowest in the evening, you may find it less of a struggle in the morning when you feel refreshed. Pencil in your planned activities in a specific time-slot in the next day's DAD – so, instead of thinking, 'I'll sort out that wardrobe and throw away some old clothes tomorrow,' put that activity in a time-slot.

2 Get the balance right. Perfectionists and people whose Rules include always doing eveything to 110 per cent of their ability may be tempted to fill the day with achievement-based activities. But missing out pleasure is the quickest way to burn out and lower your mood. And you know how damaging that can be – low mood can affect the way you think, making you focus on the negative and turning up the volume on your self-critical voice. A completely pleasure-focused schedule is, of course, just as unbalanced. It's fine to devote special days to having a good time or to complete relaxation, but on the whole, feeling that you have achieved something, or done something useful with your time, improves your feelings of self-worth and enhances the enjoyment you get from your 'pleasure' activities.

3 Record what you actually do. If you've written your plans for the day in pencil, fill in what actually happened beside that, in ink. Make sure you rate each activity for Pleasure and Achievement as usual.

4 Review your day. Before you go to bed, look over your plan and see how far you managed to stick to it. If you did something different to what you had planned, can you work out why? Maybe you planned too much to start with, or something came up that you hadn't predicted. Your aim was a balance between enjoyment and feelings of satisfaction – did you get it right? Or was there too much of one and not enough of another? Use it as food for thought for tomorrow. Remember, you're not trying to create the perfect day – just one that makes you happy!

Tips for making this work

- **Keep fine-tuning.** If your plan is realistic, balanced, and brings a sense of accomplishment as well as pleasure to your day, then you may have cracked it! If there's a 'template' that works well for you, feel free to repeat it. But bear in mind the best plans are flexible, allowing you to find space for new interests or things that need doing – do you want to get more exercise or spend more time with your teenage son? Do you want to nurture a new relationship, or start an evening class in a language you've always wanted to learn?
- **Learn from what doesn't work.** You can learn just as much from a plan that doesn't work out as you can from the 'perfect' plan. Supposing, for example, you planned to do some work on a distance-learning course from 8 p.m. to 10 p.m., but your partner persuaded you to share a bottle of wine and watch TV instead. Or supposing you planned to go for a walk before breakfast, but you turned off the alarm and went back to sleep instead. There's much to be learned from both of these experiences. Do you make a habit of changing your plans to please other people, or because you feel you *ought* to? (Did you feel selfish for not planning to devote the evening to your partner?) Did you expect too much of yourself in planning to get up at 6.30 a.m. – are you simply not a morning person? Once you're aware of these potential 'red flags', you can anticipate and plan around them. (For example, if morning is your only time to

exercise, could you lay your walking kit and shoes by the bed, ready to get into as soon as you wake up, and get to bed half an hour earlier?) And what can you learn about your self-image? (Did you agree to put off your studying because you were worried your partner would think you were 'boring' if you didn't drink wine with him? Is 'I am' your Bottom Line?)

- **Explore new pleasures.** If the pleasure factor is low in your life, this is a great opportunity to explore your interests, find new passions and try out new ways of relaxing. It's easy to get out of the habit of thinking about what you do for 'fun', particularly if your life is busy and you tend to put yourself last. Make a list of everything you'd do if time were no object, and try to think big and small. What can you do that's physically active? (Slot in a 30-minute swim? Go for a walk? Join a beginner's kayaking or ju-jitsu class?) What could you do that fits into five minutes in your day? (Try a new kind of tea? Learn a five-minute relaxation technique? Join an internet forum of like-minded people?) What can you do at home? (Cook a special meal, watch a comedy DVD, or look through your old photographs?) What can you do that's sociable (Learn salsa? Volunteer at your local Scout hut? Invite friends round for coffee?) What can you do that gets you outdoors? (Do some gardening, visit a local beauty spot, cycle or walk to work?) What can you do with your children? (Fly a kite, go on a bike ride, have a picnic in the park, build something with Lego?)
- **Put killjoy thoughts aside.** Not every planned pleasure will work for you, but the only way to find out what does is to try them. Remember that taking time out for yourself means you'll be better able to care for

those who depend on you, and do your work, jobs and chores more effectively. If your day is genuinely busy with things you have to do, it can be difficult to make time for pleasure and relaxation. How can you possibly fit in even one more thing? If you're in a demanding job, or juggling work and family life, or you're a carer of young children, elderly parents or someone who is ill, or if you have a lot of community or voluntary work commitments, time for pleasure can seem an impossibility or even an indulgence. But if you never make time just for you, you'll become tired and demotivated so that, in the end, you won't be able to meet all your obligations and you may find that your health is affected. If you really have no spare time, think creatively about where you can add pleasure into your existing routine – could you shower with a beautifully scented shower-gel? Download your favourite music or a podcast of an interesting radio programme onto an MP3 player to listen to in the supermarket? Take the scenic route back to the office after a meeting? Don't let killjoy thoughts ruin your enjoyment– you're not being indulgent, you're protecting your mental health and well being.

WHY TACKLING YOUR TO-DO LIST IS GOOD FOR YOUR SELF-CONFIDENCE

Practical problems, tasks and chores can add up if you put them off, and start to undermine your self-confidence. Each time you think about the ever-mounting list of things to be done, you're receiving a message that you 'can't cope' or even that 'you're lazy'. It can make you feel you've lost control of your life. But getting a grip on problems you've

been putting off is easier than you might think, if you follow these steps:

1   Create the ultimate 'to-do' list – jot down all the jobs
    you've been putting off and the problems you've been
    avoiding.

2   Go through and number each item in order of impor-
    tance. Then put a number 1 by whatever needs to
    be done first, and so on. If you can't decide the best
    order, simply tackle them in the order you write them
    down, or number them according to how easy you
    think they'll be to do (start with the easiest).

3   Take Task 1 and break it down into tiny steps. For
    example, if your garden fence is falling down, Step
    1 might be to write down the names and numbers
    of local fencing firms from the Yellow Pages; Step 2
    – ring them and see if they can come and give you a
    quote; Step 3 – write down and compare all quotes
    given along with any other notes such as 'not avail-
    able for six weeks' or 'good local references'; Step
    4 – choose a company (or Step 4 might be discuss-
    ing it with your partner or a family member); Step
    5 – ring your chosen company and book in a time
    to get the work done. If you come across a step you
    can't do, think about what you need to get round it
    – can you get help, advice or more information from
    anywhere?

4   Watch out for anxious predictions ('You'll never
    get this sorted') and self-critical thoughts ('You are
    so useless with paperwork', 'You always put every-
    thing off until it's too late'). If it helps, write these
    thoughts down and think of alternatives ('If I tackle it

step-by-step, I'll get through it', 'I've been so busy it's no surprise I've let things slip, but I'm sorting it out now').

5   Don't forget to include the task in your Daily Activity Diary and give it a P and an A rating.

6   Tell yourself 'Well done'! Give yourself credit for ticking off one thing on your to-do list, or making the first step towards doing it.

7   Take the next task in the list and break it down into small steps in the same way.

ESSENTIAL TAKE-HOME MESSAGES FROM THIS CHAPTER

- **Self-acceptance isn't about being big-headed.** It's about recognising your individual skills, talents and good points and bringing balance into your life so that as well as being aware of your weak points and limitations, you're also aware of the flipside of the coin.
- **This process will enhance your life, not limit it.** Self-acceptance, and learning to appreciate who you are and what you're good at, will feed your motivation to achieve, not kill it. And increasing your awareness of what's great about you will improve your relationships, not lose you friends – people are naturally drawn to those among us who have truly accepted themselves in a balanced and healthy way.
- **Daily planning helps.** Planning your day to include more pleasure, and more tasks that bring a sense

of achievement, is an important step on the journey towards self-acceptance.

Life Lesson

Making time (however small) for some pleasure in your life every day is essential, not an indulgence or an optional extra.

7

CHANGING YOUR RULES FOR LIVING

It's time to do some more digging. So far, you've looked at how negative beliefs about yourself, your personal Bottom Line, lie at the heart of your low self-confidence and may have done so since childhood. You've seen how anxious predictions and self-critical thoughts feed into that Bottom Line and keep it going strong in the present day. Now it's time to tackle another major barrier that stands between you and a balanced, healthy, confident self-image. It's the Rules for Living that you gradually put in place for yourself as you grew up, the strategies you adopted to make you 'acceptable', given your belief that you are 'inferior' or 'unlovable,' or that 'your feelings aren't as important as other people's' or that you're 'different and an outsider', or you're 'stupid' or 'useless'.

You developed your Rules for Living as a sort of personal suit of armour. They are designed both to protect you from anxious, painful feelings (such as rejection or humiliation), and also to help you appear a worthwhile person in the eyes of the outside world. Rules can also work like an escape clause – a way round the 'awful truth' of your Bottom Line. For example, at heart, you might believe yourself to be incompetent. But *so long as* you work very hard all the time and set yourself very high standards, you can override your sense of incompetence and feel OK about yourself. Or you might believe yourself to be unattractive. But *so long as* you are always the life and soul of the party, maybe no one will notice and you can feel OK about yourself.

Rules like these often work very well much of the time. For long periods, it may be possible to maintain your good opinion of yourself by obeying your Rules. But the truth is that rather than protecting you, they're actually an integral link in the vicious circle that stops your self-confidence from flourishing. Rules may mask the 'real truth' about you – or, rather, what you think is the real truth – but they don't change it. And as soon as you break your Rule (you missed a work deadline, you lost your temper), or feel you're about to, your Bottom Line springs into life ('You're not good enough!' 'You're unlovable!').

Tackling Rules for Living is like pulling out the roots of your lack of self-confidence, rather than just chopping down its branches. Finding those roots can be tricky, as can getting rid of them when they're deeply embedded – it takes effort and persistence. But by doing this you can rid yourself of those thorny bushes of anxious predictions and self-critical thinking.

In this chapter, you will learn . . .

- Where your Rule (or Rules) for Living come from and what they are.
- How your Rules for Living hold you back from developing healthy self-confidence.

- How you can replace your Rules with guiding principles that will support self-acceptance and self-respect and help you grow.

WHERE DO RULES FOR LIVING COME FROM?

The first place you learn Rules is simply by observing the actions and behaviour of your parents, or the family or carers around you as a child, from the most basic messages: 'If I smile, daddy smiles back at me', 'If I cry, mummy picks me up', to more complex ones: 'If I keep asking mummy to help me, she gets cross', 'If I fall over, nana gives me a biscuit.' Children notice what wins praise and what brings criticism, what makes their parents smile and what makes them frown. All these experiences build into a set of personal Rules that have a long-time impact on how they live their lives.

Not all Rules are unhelpful – indeed, some will save you from serious harm ('Always look both ways before crossing the road' or 'Always check the temperature of the bath water before jumping in'). But Rules work best when they're flexible and allow you to adapt to different circumstances and social situations. What is unhelpful is when Rules are rigid, and seen as *the only right way to behave*. When your personal Rules for Living are rooted in your negative beliefs about yourself, they're unhelpful.

Unhelpful Rules create restrictions on your life that hold you back from fulfilling your potential. They set you up to fail by placing impossible demands on you, by unrealistically applying the same rigid standard to every situation ('You must *always* be self-sufficient and expect no help from anyone', 'You must *never* offend people by saying what you really think', 'Your house must look *perfectly* tidy *at all times'*, 'You must *never* let anyone know you're not coping'). Although your Rules originally developed as a defence mechanism, inflexible Rules make life *more* difficult rather than easier, and create problems that simply wouldn't be there if the Rule wasn't in place. The effort involved in sticking to these Rules drains energy that you might otherwise apply elsewhere – to something more productive, fulfilling or creative – so they hold you back from achieving your true potential.

Your Rules may also be way out of date! They may well have been made before you had a chance to experience the world. They were based on a limited view of what's right and wrong, what's normal and what's not, and what are reasonable expectations of a human being. They probably made perfect sense at the time, but now that your world has expanded, they just don't fit any more.

Sometimes, Rules are shaped by the world around you. They are sometimes an exaggerated version of messages you picked up in your childhood or ones you're picking up now – 'I'm nothing if I don't have a partner', 'The more money you have, the more successful you are', 'Only white people get the best jobs', 'Being a good Christian/Muslim means putting yourself last.'

Rules that feed into your low self-confidence can manifest themselves in all areas of your life. Jackson's Rule of avoiding criticism put him under intense pressure at work, as he felt he could never admit to not knowing an answer. They can also influence your relationships. Anna's Rule of 'being self-sufficient, and expecting nothing from other people' meant she had very low expectations of relationships and often put up with being treated fairly badly. Kevin's Rule of not trying anything unless he was sure he could do it meant he stayed in a low-paid job that didn't make full use of his capabilities.

FIVE THINGS YOU NEED TO KNOW ABOUT RULES

1 Your set of Rules are yours alone. Your Rules may have much in common with those of other people growing up in the same culture, but you are the only who has experienced life in exactly the way you have. Even within the same family, every child has a different experience. So your Rules are unique to you.

2 Rules resist change. Rules affect your vision of the world like a pair of invisible glasses. And you've got so used to wearing them that it's difficult for you to see just how warped their vision is. Think back to the work you did on anxious predictions. In Chapter 4, we discovered that the precautions you take when you go into 'anxious prediction' mode actually work *against* you rather than protecting you, because they prevent you from ever finding out whether your fears are justified. The same sort of thing happens with Rules. So long as you are looking at the world through your 'Rules' glasses, and feel compelled to act accordingly, you'll never know if this vision is accurate, helpful or actually hindering you, and whether you'd actually see clearer without them.

3 Rules evoke powerful emotions. There's nothing mild about the emotions evoked by breaking one of your Rules, or when you feel you're at risk of doing so. You don't merely feel worried, you feel frightened and anxious; you don't feel irritated, you feel angry; and you don't just feel sad, you feel depressed, even despairing. The emotions are so powerful because breaking your Rules activates your Bottom Line. And it's difficult to be detached and observe what's going on when you're caught up in this maelstrom.

4 Rules are unreasonable. Rules masquerade as helpful guidelines but in reality they're completely off-kilter. They don't reflect the way other people are getting along, or what is normal and reasonable to expect of the average person. As well as making completely unrealistic demands, they work on over-generalisations. They make no concessions for changes in circumstance or situation. Rules only work in black-and-white – they don't even register shades of grey.

5 Rules crush self-confidence. Rules mean that your self-worth comes with strings attached. They mean that you can't feel good about yourself until you've ticked some impossible boxes (achieving perfection, always being in full control of your life, being liked by everyone you come into contact with). Living by your Rules means your self-confidence depends on things staying the same – always being young and attractive, being the right weight and shape, being easily successful at what you do, having a big enough house and the right kind of car, having children that are doing well, being needed by a partner. But none of these things are stable – we all get older, we get ill, we may be made redundant, our relationships may break down. Few things in life are permanent fixtures. If you can only feel good about yourself in a fixed set of circumstances, you will have a fragile self-confidence. Your aim is instead to be happy with yourself, just as you are, whatever is happening in your life and the world around you.

IDENTIFYING YOUR PERSONAL RULES FOR LIVING

It's time to get down to the nitty-gritty and identify the Rules that you live by. This can be hard work, as you may never have put them into words before. Rules can be less easy to spot than anxious predictions or self-critical thoughts. But pinning down your Rules can be the key to finding out what's feeding your low self-confidence, and what's holding you back from being the person you think you were meant to be. By uncovering your Rules for Living, you are putting down on paper what you consider you have to do, or be, so that you can feel good about yourself – the things your self-confidence depends on. You'll also have the chance to explore how these Rules prevent you from having a secure sense of personal worth.

And it can be fun! It's often fascinating to look for clues that suggest what your Rules are, and then gradually reveal them. It may even surprise you to discover what your Rules are, and you may not even believe some of them when you are calmly looking at them written down on the page. The point is that even if you're not convinced by your Rule in the cold light of day ('I must be liked by everyone'), if you act as if it were true (you hate getting on the wrong side of anyone and will go out of your way to avoid conflict), then that's a Rule in operation.

The good news is that the work you've already put in to identify your anxious predictions and self-critical thoughts means you should have a good base of information about yourself to work with. You know which situations stir up strong emotions or self-critical thoughts. These situations are relevant to your own personal set of Rules.

You may have already spotted a pattern to the situations when you feel most threatened, which will give you some big pointers towards your Rules. But don't be surprised if you still feel in the dark, or are not 100 per cent convinced that you *do* have Rules. They can be elusive and you might need a while to pin them down and find the right words to express them. In the rest of this chapter, you'll find food for thought to help you look from all angles, experiment with different words, try out ideas and follow up hunches. Your aim is to uncover those Rules that have had the biggest influence on your life so far.

The language of Rules

Rules for Living are usually expressed in one of three ways:

'If . . . , then . . .' statements. 'If someone puts me down, they must have a good reason.' 'If I say what I think, people will ridicule me.' 'If I try to get close to someone, they'll see how unlovable I am and reject me.' Another way of saying this is 'Unless . . . , then . . .' – 'Unless I keep control of what I eat every day, I can't feel good about myself.' These are known as assumptions, and describe what you think will happen if you act (or fail to act) in a certain way.

'Should', 'must' or 'ought'. 'I must never let anyone see the real me.' 'I should do everything 110 per cent.' These are known as drivers, and they force you to act in a particular way, or be a certain type of person. There's usually a hidden 'or else' lurking somewhere, as in 'I must never let anyone see the real me, or else they will see how boring I am and reject me.'

Value judgements. 'It's foolish to try things you're not qualified to do.' 'Being overweight is shameful.' 'It's essential to stand on your own two feet.' These are vaguer Rules that need a little unpicking to get to the heart of the matter. The clue lies in the descriptive words such as 'foolish', 'shameful' or 'essential'. Ask yourself, what's foolish about giving something a go? What's the worst that can happen? What do I mean by shameful? If I imagine being ashamed, what exactly comes to mind? How would I feel? What does 'essential' mean? What would happen if I wasn't completely self-sufficient? What does self-sufficiency protect me from? What is the worst that could happen if I had to ask for help? What sort of person would that make me?

RULE OR RULES?

Some people have one, all-powerful, Rule for Living, others have more than one. For example, you might feel that 'I must be liked by everyone or I am worthless', but you're also ruled by 'I must cope with everything that's thrown at me.' You should be able to uncover all your Rules in turn, finding and experimenting with acting on each one until you feel comfortable with it and ready to move onto the next rule.

SIX CLUES TO YOUR RULE

Some of these clues will lead to more information than others, but it's worth testing each one out to see what you get from it.

Clue No 1: Your favourite fears and put-downs

Look through the record you've kept of your self-critical thoughts and anxious predictions. Can you detect rules masquerading as fears or predictions? Are any of your self-critical thoughts specific examples of a more general Rule? E.g. 'You messed up *again*!' may suggest a Rule of 'If I make a mistake, it's my fault.'

Clue No 2: Look for themes

Can you pick out continuing preoccupations and concerns in your worksheets? What themes run through the work you've done so far? What kind of situations reliably make you doubt yourself (for example, noticing you've not done something well, or having to encounter people you're unfamiliar with)? What aspects of yourself are you most hard on? What behaviour in other people undermines your confidence? Repeating themes can give you some idea of what you require of yourself, of other people and of the world in general, in order to maintain your sense of self-confidence.

Clue No 3: Your judgements of yourself and other people

Look at your self-critical thoughts – under what circumstances do you begin to put yourself down? What do you criticise in yourself? What does that tell you about what you expect of yourself? What might happen if you relax your standards? How could things go wrong? If you don't keep a tight rein on yourself and obey the Rule, where will you end up? What sort of person might you become (e.g. stupid, lazy, selfish)? What are you never allowed to do, or to be, no matter what? Consider, too, what you criticise in other people. What standards do you expect them to meet? These can sometimes reflect standards you place on yourself – if you expect 110 per cent of yourself at work, you may find it hard not to disapprove of colleagues who come in late or take a much more relaxed attitude all round.

Clue No 4: Back in the day

Messages you received 'back in the day' (as a child or teenager) about how you should behave, or the kind of person you ought to be – these can rear their ugly heads as Rules!

As a child, it's easy to take things literally, or misunderstand the meaning of what's being said to you. If your parents taught you to say please by responding to your requests with 'I Want Doesn't Get', you may well have drawn the conclusion that it was wrong to want things, and that if you asked for something in a direct way it would be taken away. You may have decided that you could only get what you wanted by roundabout means, or that you should try not to want anything at all.

Now, your immediate reaction may be that you remember little about your childhood in enough detail to be helpful. If so, try looking through the **Inner critic worksheet**. Pick out some thoughts and feelings that seem typical to you (themes), then see if you can pinpoint a time when those feelings started, or when you first started thinking or behaving in the way you've noted. Look at the situations that trigger anxious predictions or self-critical thoughts – do they remind you of anything in your past? Can you hear a voice, or see a face, or do you bring to mind particular memories or images? Anna, for example, has a clear image of one occasion when her mum told her to stop making up stories to get herself out of trouble, when she came home from school and reported that some older boys would wipe mud on her coat during play-times. Later, she remembers telling her mum about the 'funny feelings' (of anxiety) she'd get on arrival at school. Her mother laughed and said 'You do have some silly ideas,' and Anna's 'funny feelings' became a family joke. Not surprisingly, Anna's Rules for Living reflected these experiences: 'I must be self-sufficient and expect no help from anyone.'

If you're having problems bringing the past into sharp focus, then try this exercise. Take some time to relax and think yourself back to a significant point in your childhood – maybe it's the age you always go back to in your dreams, or one that conjures up the clearest images. Now, picture that child sitting on a chair, and finishing these sentences:

- 'In our family, it's bad to . . .'
- 'It's very important that I always . . .'
- 'I get a lot of attention when I . . .'
- 'I always get into trouble if I . . .'
- 'If I'm bad at school, when I get home . . .'
- 'When I don't do as I'm told, the grown-ups tell me that I'm . . . or that . . . will happen.'
- 'The last time I let my family down, I was told that . . .'
- 'The best way of getting a hug or some affection at home is to . . .'
- 'Our favourite family sayings are . . .'

Clue No 5: Learn from the positive

Sometimes clues to your Rules are hidden in the good times. Even people with very low self-confidence feel good about themselves sometimes, and those times can often be a sign that you've obeyed all your Rules, or your most important Rule. Try to remember the last time you felt great – why did you feel so good? What are the implications of this? If you felt great because you looked stunning, is your Rule connected to your looks? If you finished a project and it exceeded your very high standards, what Rules did you obey? If you were on a high for days after being the life and soul of a party, do your Rules revolve around being liked by everyone?

Alternatively, if you're having trouble recalling a feel-good event, think about someone you really admire instead, someone who you have on a 'pedestal' and look up to. What is it about them that you admire so much? What Rule could it reflect in you? Or if you have a favourite day-dream about your fantasy life, what could that day-dream be saying about the way you're supposed to act or be?

Clue No 6: Use a downward arrow

This exercise focuses on a specific problem, and unpicks your reaction to it to uncover the underlying Rules. Here's how to do it.

1   Choose a starting point. Think of a situation that always upsets you and is guaranteed to make you feel bad about yourself (for example, having a disagreement with someone, losing your temper, or eating too much in public). That will be a situation where your Bottom Line is activated by the risk that you'll break your Rules, or where you have actually broken a Rule. Choose a recent episode that's still sharp in your memory.

2   Go over the details. Divide a blank sheet of paper into two columns – one headed 'Emotions', and the other 'Thoughts'. Write down everything that occurred to you under each heading. Include images under the 'Thoughts' heading. See if you can identify the thought that packs the greatest emotional punch.

3   Hold that thought! You're now going to ask a series of questions that will distil your thought down to its purest form. Supposing your thought was 'I embarrassed myself in front of everyone by drinking too much.' Start with 'Supposing that were true, what would it mean to me?' Answer the question (e.g. 'That I had lost control'). Now, ask the question again: 'And supposing that were true, what would it mean

to me?' ('That people would know I'm not perfect.')
Ask again: 'Supposing that were true, what would it
mean to me? ('That they would despise me.') If you
have a sense of going round in circles after a certain
point, chances are that you have reached your Rule
(e.g. 'I have to be perfect to be liked').

4 If that question doesn't work for you, use the technique with a different question. Some people prefer
to ask 'What's the worst that might happen? And
what would happen then? And then?' But you could
also try 'How would that be a problem for me?' or
'What does that tell me about the sort of person I
should be to feel good about myself?' or 'What does
that tell me about what I must do, or be, in order
to succeed in life?' or 'What does that tell me about
my standards?'

The power of the right question

The internationally successful self-help guru Byron Katie
has built a whole career on a version of the 'downward
arrow' exercise. She calls it 'The Work'. You simply write
down a thought that is causing you stress or suffering,
then ask yourself four questions about it: Is it true? Can I
absolutely know it's true? How do I react when I believe
this thought? Who would I be without the thought? The
aim is to replace the thought with a 'turnaround' – an
opposite thought, one that is 'as true or truer' and that
doesn't cause you suffering.

TEST-DRIVING YOUR RULE

When you think you've got a rough draft of your Rule for Living, or one of your Rules, it's time to give it a test-drive. Even if you're not quite convinced by it, see how it fits into your life. Does your Rule provide any insight into why you act as you do in certain situations? Keeping your draft Rule in the back of your mind, see if any 'Aha!' moments emerge over the next few days. Has it given you a new insight into your anxious predictions or your self-critical thoughts? Then you may have found your Rule (or one of them). Don't worry too much about the language – it may take a while to get the right wording. Read through *The language of Rules* again (a few pages back) and try out a different format. But if your Rule still doesn't seem to fit, then keep looking.

IT'S TIME TO CHANGE YOUR RULES

Rules for Living are insidious things. They quietly exert their influence 24/7, affecting the way you think, feel and act. And they may have been doing this for many, many years.

Perhaps you already have an insight into the impact that your Rule has had on your life. Taking some time to look at this in detail is the first step to change. It'll also help you come up with an alternative, a new helpful Rule that feels right for you.

Now that you have your Rule in mind, does it explain why you act a certain way in relationships? Or keep repeating the same negative patterns? Could it explain why you don't feel you deserve a relationship, or you have an urge to push away anyone who gets close? Is your Rule the reason why you find it so hard to ask for what you need, or talk about what you're really feeling?

And how is your Rule affecting your relationship with *yourself*? Does it explain why you find it so hard to put yourself first, and give your mind and body the care and attention it deserves? Is your Rule stopping you from being the person you feel you could be, whether that's slimmer or fitter, more successful, or simply happier and more fulfilled? How often do you find yourself riding a wave of uncomfortable thoughts, emotions and physical symptoms because your Rule has been broken, or is at risk of being broken? How much mental energy do you use coping with this and trying to go about your daily life as if nothing were happening?

Looking back in time, can you see how your Rule influenced your personality as you grew up? Has it made you more cautious and self-protective? You already know it's affected your self-confidence, but did it also dampen your natural sense of humour, or your ability to relax around other people? Has it made you more uptight or less creative? Does it explain why you fall into anxious-prediction mode or have a vocal inner critic?

Now you've 'named and shamed' your Rule or Rules, you may be expecting them to do the decent thing and leave. Unfortunately, the eviction process is a little more complex than that! But the good news is that you've already done a lot of the groundwork. You've learned skills for nipping anxious predictions in the bud, and shutting up your inner critic. You've embraced your good points and accepted that you deserve some pleasure in life. See how far you've come on your journey? It's all helped the scales fall from your eyes so you can see your Rule for what it really is. Now your aim is to find a *new* Rule which works *with* you, not against you. For a start, it'll be realistic, and not based on 'fantasy' standards that no one could live up to. And instead of perpetually knocking you back, it'll pick you up and gently encourage you on a positive path.

If you've discovered that you have more than one Rule, start with the one you'd most like to change and complete the process before starting on the next one. You may be tempted to work on more than one Rule at once, but you'll do a more thorough job if you make each one a solo project.

Here are the steps that will take you further.

🖊 TIME TO GET WRITING:

Changing your Rules

Seven steps to changing a Rule

Step 1: Write it down

Complete the following three statements as best you can.

- My Rule for Living is . . .
- This Rule has affected my life by . . .
- I know I'm trying to follow my Rule when I find myself . . .

Step 2: Record your 'back story'

This is the first step in the detachment process – switching from unconsciously following your Rule, to simply observing it. You're going to take a detailed look at the more negative aspects of your past, but this isn't some kind of pity party! Tracing the roots of your Rule is a way of demystifying it and taking away its power. The work you've done so far will have already given you insight into where your Rule came from – and why it seemed like a good thing at the time. You've already collected a lot of the jigsaw pieces, so now it's time to put them all together.

Writing your Rule's 'back story' will help you consolidate all the information you've amassed so far. You may have a mix of insights, theories and snapshots from the past buzzing around your brain – it's time to pin them down on paper before they start to fade. It doesn't have to be an essay – just use bullet points or a list (or a stream of consciousness if you work better that way). Your aim is to record all the experiences that lead you to believe that you *needed* the Rule. Can you trace the birth of the Rule to one specific difficult time? Can you write down the very first time you changed your behaviour to keep in line with the Rule? Or your first realisation that your family, society or culture expected you to follow the Rule? And what about people and relationships – who were the main characters in the story and what part did they play in making you feel that you needed the Rule to survive, or be lovable or acceptable? What did they say and do?

Now fast-forward to more recent years. What adult experiences have helped convince you that you need to live by your Rule? Have you had relationships – either intimate or professional – with people that have reinforced your belief in the Rule? Have you found yourself drawn to a certain type of person – demanding, needy, abusive, dismissive? Is there a pattern to your relationships? If one adult helped create the Rule as a child, have you replaced them with a partner or boss who treats you in a similar way?

The point of this exercise is not to make you feel like a victim for letting someone get to you, or a loser for deciding you weren't as good as anyone else. Remember, your Rule was a survival strategy – it's how you got by in day-to-day life, or how you made sense of the confusing world around you. *And it was perfectly understandable, given the circumstances at the time.* But now is the time to ask, do I *still* need this Rule? Is this Rule still helping me? Or is it time for an update?

Step 3: Look at why the Rule stinks!

Don't hold back – it's time for a complete character assignation! Does your Rule set you up to fail? Does it expect you to act like a superhuman at all times? Is it completely inflexible, taking no account of changing circumstances? Is it simply over-the-top in its demands? Or is it just blatantly out of date?

Would you recommend your Rule to someone you love? If not, then why do you expect it from yourself? Bear in mind, you put this Rule in place when you were a child. Are you happy that a child is effectively running your life for you? Can you see that the decisions you made, and conclusions you came to, earlier in your life, may have been based on incomplete information, insight or life experience?

Step 4: Uncover the positives

Rules for Living always have pay-offs – it's partly why you hold on to them for so long. Has a Rule about always putting in 110 per cent effort earned you a reputation as a grafter at work? Does a Rule about always putting others first mean people think you're a nice person, or even a 'saint'? Does a Rule about coping and never complaining mean you keep the family going, whatever you have to deal with? Or has a Rule of always being the best at everything you do driven you up the career ladder, or kept you striving for academic success?

Thinking positively about your Rule may feel like a backward step, but it's important to be clear about what you gain from your Rule. Recovering alcoholics know that they need to replace the positives they get from drinking – like being able to relax and switch off – if they're going to stay off the booze long-term. It's a bit like that with Rules. You won't be able to let go of your unhelpful Rule unless you can come up with an alternative that brings the same benefits.

So jot down what you think are *your* pay-offs, the advantages of your Rule (e.g. It makes me feel useful; It means I never have to deal with conflict). What worries you about giving up your Rule? What do you think you'd be at risk from (e.g. I'd never get anywhere in life; I'd be criticised at work)? Once you've got them down in black-and-white, move on to Step 5.

Step 5: List the downsides

When you've listed all the pay-offs of your Rule, you're going to take a careful look at them and assess just how helpful they really are. For example, the Rule that you must never complain may go down well at work, and earn you a reputation for being 'low maintenance'. But does it leave you seething with resentment? Do you come home and head for the fridge or biscuit tin to soothe your emotions and lift your mood? Or has it meant you regularly get dumped with extra work because your boss knows you won't make a fuss? Does your Rule of 'coping with everything' have a negative effect on your relationships because the people close to you often feel a bit redundant? Has your Rule of never making demands on anyone, never asking for what you need in relationships, meant your friendships tend to be one-sided, or never get past the casual stage?

Even when you think your Rule is helping you, there's a good chance it's actually doing the opposite, and holding you back from opportunities. You may thank your 'I must be perfect at everything' Rule for where you are today, but just think where you could be if you'd worked *smarter* – and applied all your energy in the right direction – instead of simply working *harder* at everything. If you're sure your 'I must never let anyone see the real me' Rule has helped you make friends, have you considered how many potential friends or partners have been baffled or turned off by your carefully controlled, two-dimensional image? And are you *sure* people approve of your 'I must put myself last' Rule? Could it actually come across as a bit martyrish?

Now, let's look at the mental wish-list that we all carry around in our heads. Try writing it down as a list of sentences that start with 'I'd like to . . .' For example, 'I'd like to lose 40 lbs', 'I'd like to find a supportive partner and start a family', 'I'd like a more creative job', 'I'd like to feel more relaxed about talking to people'. Now, look at each one in turn and ask, is my Rule *really* helping me achieve this? If so, then why is it still a goal, and not reality? If your Rule hasn't helped so far, isn't it worth trying something different, and seeing what happens *without* the Rule?

If you're still convinced your Rule has valuable pay-offs, try this version of a 'pros and cons' exercise. Take a sheet of paper and draw a vertical line down the middle. In the left-hand column, write down the positives that you feel you get from your Rule, and what you'd lose or would happen if you gave your Rule up. In the right-hand column, list its disadvantages. Which side is the most convincing? If the disadvantages of the Rule outweigh the advantages, then you need to update it. That doesn't mean you'll lose the positive pay-offs, but you need to find a way of benefiting from them without paying such a high personal cost.

Step 6: Think of a more helpful alternative Rule

Imagine feeling quietly confident when faced with challenging situations, or just slightly apprehensive rather than gripped by anxiety. Would you like to have an internal commentary that told you how well you were doing under the circumstances, and encouraged you to keep going? Would you like to face problems without panic, and treat them as inconveniences to be dealt with, rather than disasters? Swapping your old Rule for a better one can help you do this.

We've already discussed that your new Rule should provide as many of the positive pay-offs – that is, the genuinely positive pay-offs – as the old Rule did. But what's important is that it's a flexible rather than a one-size-fits-all Rule – it must be adaptable so that it's still useful, even when your situations and circumstances change. So all-or-nothing, black-and-white Rules are out. The words that describe it will be 'I want . . .', 'I enjoy . . .', 'I prefer . . .', or 'It's OK to . . .', rather than 'I must . . .', 'I should . . .', 'I ought to . . .', or 'It would be terrible if . . .'. Have another look at *The language of Rules*. Your new Rule might begin in the same way as the old one ('If . . .'), but continue with a different 'then . . .'. For example, you could swap, 'If someone criticises me, I must have deserved it,' for 'If someone criticises me, that could mean I deserved it, but not necessarily. And if I have done something that it would be fair to criticise, it doesn't mean I've failed, it just means I'm human like everyone else.'

If you're having a mental block, imagine the kind of Rule you'd advise someone to live by, if they asked. 'I enjoy meeting and being with other people, but I don't expect everyone I meet to like me.' 'It's OK to aim for "good enough" sometimes, not 110 per cent.' Or can you think of an updated version of your Rule that you'd be happy to pass on to your children? 'Being the best I can, under the circumstances, at the things that are important to me, will get me further in life than trying to be perfect at everything.'

Don't worry if your new Rule is longer or more complex than your old Rule – this is a good sign. It means the new Rule is multi-dimensional and is based on a deeper understanding of how things work in the real world. But if you're motivated by punchy, snappy sayings, then try to distil it down into a phrase you can use like a mantra. 'I am who I am, and that's OK.' 'Good enough is better than perfect.' 'I have to love myself before I can love another.'

Don't spend hours wrestling with it. Write down a rough idea, then try living with it for a week or two to see how it fits, or if you need to tweak it – or try a completely new Rule altogether.

Step 7: Put your new Rule on trial

Once you're happy with your new Rule, you need to start putting it into practice. Eventually, you'll do this without thinking, but to get you started, you need to consciously apply it to your life, and observe the results. Remember – re-thinking is only the first step, and your best teacher is direct personal experience of how things could be different. So to make sure your new Rule really does suit you, you need to try living your life *as if* you believed it (as if you believed you were just as good as anyone else; or worthy of a loving, supportive relationship; or a worthwhile person; or whatever) for a period of time, and see what happens. Read on to find out the best way to do this.

TOP TIPS FOR MAKING THIS WORK

- **Write a self-discovery 'journal'.** You don't have to post it on the Net – it's just for you. Follow the headings on page 176 (and you might find it helpful to read through Jackson's completed blog on pages 179–81). Then, every day for the next few weeks, read your journal carefully and let it sink in at least once that day, just after you get up or just before you go to bed. At the start of the day, it can put you in the right frame of mind for the day. At the end of the day, consider how the Rule is changing things for you. Your aim is to make your new Rule sink into your consciousness, so that it has the best possible chance of influencing your feelings and thoughts and how you react when the going gets tough.

- **Write it down somewhere to refer to.** Make a note of your new Rule on your phone so you can remind yourself of it when you need to. Or, write it on a small card (credit-card size) and keep it in the 'window' section of your purse or wallet, so it's there every time you pay for something, or to look at when you feel low, or you're facing a challenging situation.

- **Look out for your old Rule.** Even when you've established a good alternative and are starting to live with your new Rule, you may still feel anxious or start to worry when you do something that would have broken your old Rule. You may feel churned up for hours after you say no to your boss's last-minute request to come in and work this weekend (because you'd planned a long-overdue weekend away). Don't assume this means the technique isn't working for you, or that nothing has changed. For a start, you now have an awareness of what is causing your feelings, which means you're better able to be objective about it. You can say to yourself, 'I'm feeling like this because my old Rule didn't allow me to say no, or to put myself first, not because it's wrong to turn down weekend working for a good reason.' Sometimes, it will be enough simply to say to yourself, 'There's that old out-of-date Rule of mine.' At other times, you may need to a bit of a pep-talk – perhaps by re-reading the notes you made on your Rule's pros and cons, why it's out of date, what your new Rule is and why it will help you achieve your goals or just feel happier. In time, you should find you get over this stage without much bother.

- **Be specific.** For this to work, you need a plan. So don't just think that you'll 'give up trying to be super-woman'. You need to decide that you'll go to bed without tidying the house when you're tired, let the family eat beans on toast when you don't have time to cook, and swap one 'duty' activity a day for a treat. Then take a look at your Daily Activity Diary and see where these changes could fit in, like a series of mini-experiments. Then, observe how your new behaviour made you feel about yourself, how other people reacted and how that made you feel. See whether on the whole it suggests your new Rule is right for you (or not).

- **Give yourself a break.** Acting as if you believe your new Rule is true can feel uncomfortable at first. You may start to feel guilty, worried or anxious at the thought of acting in a new way (such as being less self-sacrificing, or expressing your true feelings). If this happens, can you tell what it is you're predict-ing might happen (the other person will shout at you, you'll end up in an argument, you'll be rejected)? If so, you can try a mini-experiment to check it out. For example, the next time your partner puts you down in public, decide that when you're next alone you'll tell him that you don't appreciate it, you don't deserve it, and it's embarrassing for everyone else who's there. But don't get angry with yourself and become self-critical if you plan to carry out an experiment, and then find you can't go through with it. Don't give yourself a hard time, or assume you're back where you started. It's natural for changing old habits to be difficult or even scary, especially if they've been around for a long time and have had some advantages. Be kind to yourself when things are hard and, if you can, use what you've learned to discover the thoughts behind the uncomfortable feelings (e.g. 'you'll be rejected if you speak your mind'). Question them, and look for alternatives that are likely to be more helpful to you and that you can check out, such as 'he may get defensive, but if he loves me, he'll try to change'.

- **Don't give up.** Be aware that it can take as long as six to eight months for a new Rule to feel second-nature. But as the poster slogan says, 'Keep calm, and carry on.' Stay motivated by reminding yourself how far you've come. You could use targets to keep yourself motivated.

- **Keep written records.** The best way to keep track of your progress is to do the exercises in this book and fill out the worksheets as you do them. Make copies of the sheets and fill in as many as you can. Take a look back at the work you've done whenever you feel you need a boost or a pat on the back.

My Journal – Changing the Rules

My old Rule is:

This Rule has had the following impact on my life:

I know I'm living with this Rule because:

Where the Rule came from:

Why the Rule is unreasonable:

The pay-offs of my Rule are:

Its disadvantages are:

A more realistic, flexible, helpful Rule would be:

In order to test-drive the new Rule, I need to:

Changing the Rules: Jackson's journal

My old Rule is: 'I must do everything 110 per cent, or I will never get anywhere in life.'

This Rule has had the following impact on my life: Work has always come first to me. I have to feel like I'm achieving something or I can't relax. I'm always the last to leave work and the first to arrive. I know I've done well at work but I can never relax. I feel that as soon as I slack off, they'll see me for the imposter that I really am. I'm constantly on the look-out for criticism and signs my boss isn't happy with something. A lot of the time I feel incredibly stressed, to the extent that at times it's made me feel ill (not that I took a day off!). But it's hit my relationships hardest. My wife gets frustrated when I work late and then bring work home with me. She hates me bringing work on holiday. And I know I'm missing out on a lot of my children's lives because I'm never really there. But when I'm with them, it ruins things – I get cross when we play football in the garden and they don't play 'properly'. And when I help them with their home-work, I end up doing it for them, because I can't bear to see it done less than perfectly.

I know I'm living with this Rule because: I start to feel incredibly stressed and a bit panicky. I go over and over everything and sometimes stay up all night working. Then I get to work and have to rely on caffeine to keep me awake. If I feel like I've somehow not made my usual grade, I feel very depressed, like everything I've ever achieved was just a fluke, and that really I'm a failure.

Where the Rule came from: My parents believed in 'tough love', and that encouraging a child meant you were spoiling him. So instead of praising me, even when I did well, they looked for what they could criticise. They would tell me that my behaviour wasn't good enough, and that I would never get anywhere in life unless I tried harder. I know now that they were very proud of me, but I don't have a single memory of them saying that to me. Growing up, I felt like if I could just be better at everything, and do it all perfectly, then my parents would love me.

Why the Rule is unreasonable: I know in my heart-of-hearts that it's simply not possible to get it right all the time. Other people do a good job and they only put in half the effort I do. Everyone makes mistakes – why can't I? Why is 'good enough' acceptable for most people, but not for me?

The pay-offs of my Rule are: I've done well in my job and that's meant we can live in a nice home and have a good standard of living. I'm respected at work. I feel like I can look myself in the eye if I've put in 110 per cent. I feel good about myself for the rest of the day if I get feedback for a job well done.

Its disadvantages are: I feel as anxious about doing reports today as I did ten years ago, when I started this job. If there's a problem with a project that I'm overseeing, I automatically assume it's my fault, and that I've missed something. I take even casual negative comments as dire criticism and go over and over it in my head. I'm always the person who gets called at weekends if something comes up because they know I'll sort it out. Lately, I've started avoiding new challenges, just in case I can't get it absolutely right. I think people respect me, but they don't feel comfortable around me. I've been left out of a few group events lately. I seem to have fewer and fewer friends. I feel like all my time and attention is devoted to my work and it's like a treadmill that I can't get off.

A more realistic, flexible, helpful Rule would be: Sometimes good enough is enough. I'm still a worthwhile person if I give 80 per cent at times, rather than 110 per cent.

In order to test-drive the new Rule, I need to:
- Read this summary and really let it sink in.
- Make a note of my new Rule on my phone so I can remind myself of it.
- Tell my boss I intend to cut my working hours. Aim to be at home by 6.30 at least four nights a week.
- Take a morning off for the next school play.
- Take up badminton again.
- See what happens if I say 'I don't know' when I'm asked something I can't answer.
- Put negative comments and criticism into context. Treat them as something to be learned from.
- Set myself a time limit to work on my next project, and stick to it.
- Set up an office rota for out-of-hours emergencies rather than dealing with them all myself.
- Turn off my phone when I'm not on call and only answer work emails in the office.
- Watch out for signs of stress and pressure – get up and take a walk around the block when I feel the old thoughts coming back.
- Remember, good enough is enough.

ESSENTIAL TAKE-HOME MESSAGES FROM THIS CHAPTER

- Rules are learned from childhood onwards and may have been with you for years, but that doesn't mean they have to be with you for ever. You can formulate new, more realistic and helpful Rules.
- Unhelpful Rules for Living set you up to fail with unreasonable standards and impossible expectations. By expecting you to act like a superhuman, they make you feel bad for acting like a normal human being.
- Rules represent a way of coping with your Bottom

Line, but they do nothing to help change it. In fact, they help to keep it in place.

- You pay too high a price for the few positive benefits of your unhelpful Rules (if there *are* any benefits). There are easier ways to get the same pay-offs!

- You can feel good about yourself even if you're not perfect, even if some people don't like you or disapprove of the way you are, even if sometimes you prioritise your own wants and needs, even if you sometimes lose control.

Life Lesson

Do what you've always done, and you'll get what you've always got.

8

WHO WOULD YOU LIKE TO BE?

If you've been working through this book as you read it, following the exercises, you should have noticed changes taking place already. This chapter will consolidate these changes and take you one step further to make the most crucial, life-changing step of all – creating a new Bottom Line. Your new Bottom Line will take the place of those negative beliefs about yourself that lie at the heart of your self-confidence and have dictated how you think, feel and act for long enough.

If there's a small voice in your head, doubting whether this will ever be possible, take a minute to review just how far you've come. Here are the foundations you've already laid for tackling your Bottom Line.

- In Chapter 2, you learned how your negative beliefs developed. Although it was understandable that you reached those conclusions, given your experiences, you know now that they are not facts, but *opinions*! Negative thinking, or biases in the way you perceive and interpret what happens to you, keeps these conclusions alive and kicking. To help you cope with life and feel better about yourself, you developed certain Rules for Living, which, in the long run, have done more harm than good, and have fed your insecurities and poor self-image.

- In Chapter 3, you discovered that you predict the worst when you feel you're in danger of breaking your personal Rules for Living, and these anxious predictions can trigger self-critical thoughts.

- In Chapter 4, you learned how to question your anxious predictions and test them out for yourself instead of automatically accepting that what you predict will be accurate.

- In Chapter 5, you learned how to turn down the volume on your inner critic, that mental soundtrack that just keeps your mood and your confidence low.

- In Chapter 6, you learned how planning some pleasure and a sense of achievement into every day is essential for strengthening your self-confidence.

- In Chapter 7, you learned why your Rules for Living are out of date, how they hold you back from achieving your full potential, and how to update them so they're more flexible, helpful and realistic.

You may already feel more detached from your old Bottom Line than you did when you first started working through this book, because each of these achievements has chipped away at your belief in it. For some people, it's enough to break the vicious circle of anxious predictions and self-critical thoughts that keep low self-confidence going, and embrace a realistic and helpful set of Rules for Living. Other people find their negative beliefs about themselves are harder to shift, and that day-to-day changes in thinking and behaviour are more difficult to make. Whatever stage you find yourself in now, this chapter is crucial, because it will guide you through the process of replacing your old negative Bottom Line with a core belief that is positive, helpful, accurate, appreciative and supportive of what you want to achieve in life. You've almost completed your journey towards self-acceptance, and this is the last stage.

In this chapter you will . . .

- Look the enemy in the eye! By focusing on your Bottom Line, you'll learn more about your deepest negative beliefs about yourself.

- Start creating a more realistic New Bottom Line.

You may well have a pretty good idea by now of what your Bottom Line is, or it may still be proving elusive, and floating on the edge of your awareness. Now it's time to pin it down, put it into words and give it a clear definition. You'll find all the tools you need in this section.

Each exercise will give you a slightly different 'take' on things, so it's worth having a go at all of them. Each one has the potential to reveal new insights, or help you define an elusive feeling, or even uncover elements of your Bottom Line that have so far evaded your awareness.

In the previous chapter, you discovered that it's possible to have more than one Rule for Living. It's the same with your Bottom Line – you may have more than one (like Meena, who saw herself both as inferior, and as a misfit). If this is the case, tackle them one-by-one, starting with the one you most want to change, and use the chapter to work systematically through that Bottom Line. You'll find you've done a lot of groundwork when you come to tackle the next one.

✐ TIME TO GET WRITING:

Pin down your Bottom Line

Your aim by the end of this exercise is to be able to finish the following sentence: *My Bottom Line is: 'I am . . .'* and record it in the **Updating my Bottom Line worksheet** on pages 214–15 with a rating to show how much you believe it – just as you rated your anxious and self-critical thoughts.

Have you already noticed that your Bottom Line feels more believable on some days than others, depending on your mood or the situation you find yourself in? Because you've already come a long way, you may find that you only really believe your Bottom Line now when you're under a lot of pressure, or something upsetting has happened. It may be helpful to do the exercises with two ratings – one for everyday life, and one for when it's most convincing.

If you have tried out all the ideas and exercises as you worked through this book, it's highly likely that your belief in your Bottom Line has changed since you started. If so, can you rate how strongly you believed your Bottom Line *before* you started the book (8, 9, 10?), and how strongly you believe it now (1 or 2? 3?)? It's worth trying to see which part of the work you've done made the most difference. Was it becoming more aware of what makes you feel anxious, but discovering that your worst fears did not happen? Was it learning to challenge your inner critic? Was taking the time to concentrate on your positive qualities, and beginning to treat yourself like someone who deserves the good things in life? Or was it questioning and updating your new Rules for Living and then trying them on for size? Perhaps it was a bit of everything. It's a good idea to identify what's worked for you so far, so you know how to keep making progress in the future.

When your belief in your Bottom Line changes, the emotions (sadness, depression, worry, guilt, desperation) will change too. You may find that the feelings it creates when you focus on it are far less intense than when you first picked this book up. This is another sign that you're well on your way. But if you get an emotional 'block' when you start this exercise, here are some clues to help you.

SIX CLUES TO HELP IDENTIFY YOUR BOTTOM LINE

Clue No 1: Your personal history

You know by now that your past played a major role in your lack of self-confidence. Now it's time to bring your key memories, event and experiences together, and see if you can distil the essence of them into a Bottom Line. What memories jump out of your childhood and teenage years? What happened to make you feel you were lacking in some way as a person? Can you pinpoint a specific time in your life when your feelings about yourself changed (e.g. starting a new school, or your parents splitting up)? Whose voice do you hear in your head when you're being hard on yourself? What do they say?

Clue No 2: Your anxious predictions

Have a look at the work you did on your anxious predictions for Chapter 4. The fears that underlie your predictions, and what you do to stop these fears coming true, will give you clues about your Bottom Line. Supposing the worst had happened – what sort of person would that have made you? Tara's worst fears, for example (pages 64–6), were being given the cold shoulder by her friends. She made sure it never happened by avoiding social events so her friends never found out what she was 'really like'. Her Bottom Line was that she was boring.

Look at what *you* do to make sure your anxious predictions don't come true (your safety-seeking behaviours). If your anxieties are centred around the impression you make on other people, your precautions may well have been designed to hide the 'real you'. If so, *what* 'real you'? Can you describe that person you were afraid of revealing if you didn't take precautions to keep your real self hidden?

Clue No 3: Your self-critical thoughts

Look back at the work you did in Chapter 5 on challenging your inner critic. Your mental commentary has a direct connection with your Bottom Line. When you do things that trigger self-criticism, what names do you call yourself? Is there a pattern to your insults? What's the first thing that pops into your head? Can you identify what it is you believe about yourself that invites self-criticism (stupid, bad, pathetic)? Paul, for example, would call himself 'pathetic' if he tried to make conversation with an attractive woman and she didn't seem interested, because his Bottom Line was that he was unlovable.

Clue No 4: What stops you being good to yourself?

In Chapter 6, you focused on listing your good points and then observing them in action, giving yourself credit for what you do well and treating yourself with compassion. What doubts and reservations cropped up when you were working through that chapter? What mental 'stop signs' popped up when you tried to embrace the good stuff about yourself? And what beliefs about yourself do they reflect?

When Jackson tried to give himself credit for being accurate with numbers, the thought 'not quite accurate enough' kept popping into his head, because his Bottom Line was that he was 'not good enough'.

Clue No 5: Your Rules for Living

In Chapter 7, you identified your Rules for Living. In some cases, this can lead you directly to your Bottom Line. If your Rule started with 'If . . .' or 'Unless . . .', look at what you wrote after 'then . . .'. For example, 'If I make mistakes, then *I am incompetent.*'

If your Rule started 'I should . . .', look at what comes after 'or else . . .'. ('I should always be achieving something, or else *I am a loser.*')

Clue No 6: The downward arrow

If you found the downward arrow technique you learned in Chapter 7 useful for identifying your Rules for Living, you can apply it to your Bottom Line too:

- Think of one specific situation when you felt bad about yourself.
- What emotions did you feel?
- What thought was most powerful?

That's your starting point for a series of questions:

What thought was most powerful?

↓

If that thought were accurate, what would it
mean about you?

What would *that*, in turn, tell you about yourself?

So then, if *that* were true, what kind of
person would it make you?

What beliefs about yourself does it reflect?

↓

Remember, the aim is to end up with a statement that starts
'I am . . .'. If you can't get there, try starting with a different situation in which you typically feel bad about yourself.
You can see how Charlotte tackled this downward arrow
exercise in the panel.

When you think you've pinned down your Bottom Line,
add it to the **Updating my Bottom Line worksheet** on pages
214–15, and rate your belief in it from 0 to 10. The rating may vary according to situation. A rating of 10 would
mean you fully believe, 5 that you have reasonable doubts,
1 that you barely believe it at all.

Charlotte's Downward Arrows

Situation: My boss not acknowledging me in the lift
this morning

Emotions: Anxious, worried, guilty

Thought: He's obviously unhappy about something
I've done.

Suppose that was true, what would it mean about me?

That I'm not good enough at my job.

And what would that tell me about myself?

That I got this job by fluke and now he's wised up to the real me.

If he had, what kind of person would the 'real me' be?

Someone who's not heavyweight enough for the job.

If that was true, what would it mean I believed about myself as a person?

I'm an airhead, a joke.

UPDATING YOUR OLD BOTTOM LINE

You've identified your Bottom Line – now it's time to create a new one. If you're wondering why, and are thinking that surely identifying your Bottom Line is enough, think about this. Your Bottom Line is like a specially dedicated

Facebook page of negative experiences, full of pictures, comments and memories that confirm your lowest self-image. You can mentally click on the page any time you want and it's all there for you! But so far, there's no 'mental' page for your positive experiences, for the kind, supportive thoughts and memories that reflect positive aspects of yourself. You need a new page for your New Bottom Line, so you can read it as often as you need to feel good about yourself.

Creating a New Bottom Line helps shift the balance from merely contradicting your negative, old Bottom Line ('Maybe I'm not inferior') to focusing on information and experiences that support a new, positive Bottom Line ('I am just as good as anyone else'). Your New Bottom Line is instrumental in changing how you feel about yourself, shifting your thinking and your perspective on what has happened to you, to allow you to embrace and accept the good in you and your life.

You may already have an alternative Bottom Line taking shape in your mind. Look over the notes you made while working through Chapter 6 – what are your qualities, strengths, assets and skills? Can you think of a Bottom Line that takes account of these? What New Bottom Line would acknowledge your good points and put your weaknesses into perspective?

✎ *TIME TO GET WRITING:*

Creating a New Bottom Line

How to do it

When you've got a *rough idea* of your New Bottom Line, add it to the **Updating my Bottom Line worksheet** near the end of this chapter, on pages 214–15. Rate how much you believe it, just as you rated your belief in your Old Bottom Line. (Include variations if it seems more, or less, convincing to you at different times.) Then take a moment to focus your attention on it, and note what emotions come up and how strong they are. As you continue to work through this chapter, keep checking the worksheet and see how your belief in your New Bottom Line changes as you focus on the evidence that supports and strengthens it.

Tips for making this work

- **Make it personal.** What's important is that your New Bottom Line makes sense to you personally. Sometimes, a New Bottom Line is simply the opposite of the old one. For example, 'I am boring' might becomes 'I am as interesting as anyone else'; or the old 'My feelings don't count, other people's are more important' might become 'My feelings are as important as everyone else's'. But in other cases, the New Bottom Line is more complex. For example, 'I am fat and ugly' might become 'I approve of myself and don't need anyone else's approval to feel good'. Some New Bottom Lines are somewhere between these two – the exact wording must always be yours.

- **Don't force it.** Don't worry if you keep hitting a mental block. Just work through the rest of the chapter and your thoughts should start to crystallise. For the moment, try simply filling in the blanks in this sentence: 'If I wasn't. . . (fill in your Old Bottom Line here, e.g. pathetic, or unlovable), I would like to be. . . (e.g. acceptable, or likable). Then try it on for size, work through the rest of the chapter with it in mind, and see if it begins to feel comfortable. If it doesn't, try another.

- **Be realistic.** Remember, this book is about achieving a realistic view of yourself, not replacing a negative view with a unrealistically positive view from the opposite end of the spectrum! It's about accepting that your flaws and weaknesses are simply a part of you, something you may decide you can live with, or you may decide to change, but not a reason to dismiss your whole value as a person. It's obvious that being 100 per cent of anything just isn't possible. Now, think about people you know – are any of them 100 per cent likable, funny, or patient? When you decide on your New Bottom Line, keep this point in mind – it doesn't have to reflect 100 per cent, good enough is enough!

Don't worry if you've come up with a New Bottom Line but are still not completely convinced by it. If you've lived with your negative self-belief for some time, you will need time, patience and practice to make the new one feel as real. The work you've done so far has started chipping away at the foundations of your Old Bottom Line but now it's time to bring in the heavy machinery, and start to fully excavate it. Here are the five steps you need to take now:

FOUR STEPS TO CREATING A NEW BOTTOM LINE

Step 1: Reassess your old 'evidence'

It's time to re-run that personally edited DVD of yours entitled 'Reasons to believe your Bottom Line' and re-examine the evidence! Now that you know about biases in thinking and memory, can you see an alternative perspective on your 'back story'? This is not about whitewashing or rewriting the past, but about taking a step back, and an objective point of view. It's about allowing for the possibility that events in the past could be viewed differently, if approached with a new mindset.

'Evidence' that supports a Bottom Line may be purely made up of past relationships or experiences or it may be a mix of old events and more recent stuff. Whatever shape it takes, it will be unique to you. But there are some common sources of 'evidence' that crop up time and again, and they are set out below – as you look at each in detail, see which ones resonate with you.

Once you have identified the evidence that you feel backs up your Old Bottom Line, write it in the relevant section of your **Updating my Bottom Line worksheet** on pages 214–15. Then examine this evidence carefully and objectively, and see how it could be viewed differently. Record your new ways of understanding on your worksheet. Then rate how far you believe your Old and New Bottom Lines and how you feel when you consider them. Can you see a change? If so, what made the difference? If not, is there more 'evidence' you've not addressed?

Old 'evidence': Difficult times

Charlotte left college with a hefty student loan to pay off, as well as some other debts. Her first job was fairly low-paid and the city-centre flat she was renting took up most of her monthly income. She tried to juggle her overdrafts and scrape together enough money to pay the essential bills, but she was so penniless by the end of the month she'd have to walk to work. Although there were probably hundreds of other young people undergoing the same struggle, to Charlotte, it was undeniable evidence of her Bottom Line – that she was a joke. She saw the situation as a sign of her weakness as a person, rather than as a hurdle to overcome at the start of her career.

Reassess it: Problems and difficulties are usually the result of a number of factors coinciding. Sometimes, they happen for no reason at all. But they're not a sign that there is something fundamentally wrong with you, that you are inadequate, bad or whatever you're feeling. There's a whole host of high-profile, highly functioning people who have been through bad times. How would you reassess the situation if it happened to a friend? Or if you were a counsellor and a person came to see you with the problem? Think of a more compassionate and reasonable explanation of the situation.

Old 'evidence': Needing help

Do you expect to sort out all of your problems on your own, and see having to ask for help as a sign of failure, rather than just a way of getting a second opinion or of letting someone close to you feel part of your life? When Jackson's boss assigned him an intern to help him get a big project finished in time, he took it as a sign that he'd failed, or that his boss knew he wasn't up to the job. In fact, his boss thought he was doing Jackson a favour.

Reassess it: Although it's useful – at times – to be able to manage independently, asking for help is not a sign of weakness or inadequacy. Think about how you felt the last time someone came to you for help and support – did you automatically conclude they must be pathetic? Did you think less of them? Or did you think their request was reasonable or sensible? So if you've needed help in the past, why do you see that as evidence that supports your Old Bottom Line? It could, in fact, be evidence of your emotional intelligence – asking for help from people who care about you makes them feel useful and wanted!

Old 'evidence': Past failures

Unless you've lived your life in a bubble, there will have been times in the past when you've been thoughtless, embarrassing, irritating, irresponsible, dishonest or reckless. You can't be at your best every minute of the day, we're all human and have weaknesses. If you have healthy self-confidence, you'll cringe, pick yourself up, learn from the experience and move on. If you lack self-confidence, you'll use the memory as a stick to beat yourself with, and file it as 'indisputable evidence' that backs up your Old Bottom Line. Meena, for example, once drank a little too much out of nervousness at a work party, fell over on her high-heels on the dance floor, and was helped to a chair by a colleague. Needless to say, she was the butt of the office jokes about her unique 'dancing style' for the following week. Despite the fact that the jokes were lighthearted, and the event was soon old news, to Meena it was evidence that she'd never be taken seriously at work, and would never quite fit in, because she was inferior and a misfit.

Reassess it: Are you confusing what you *do*, with what you *are*? Mistakes or misguided behaviour don't mean you're a bad person. You're not a complete failure just because you've failed in the past. You're just a normal human being – we all have regrets and things we'd do differently if we had the time again. But who you are is who you are *now*, in this present moment. The past is not *part* of you, it's just something that you went through. Think of it this way – if you do one good thing, does that make you a totally good person? If that doesn't make sense, how about condemning yourself as a completely bad person due to one mistake? Rather than being evidence of the truth of your Bottom Line, can you see your past regrets as evidence that you're a normal human being? And bear in mind the context of the situation – what you did or said may have been inevitable or entirely predictable, given your situation at the time. (Who hasn't drunk a bit much, or been clumsy, out of nervousness?) Treating yourself more tolerantly doesn't mean dismissing your past mistakes as irrelevant, but it's how you begin learning a different way of thinking about them. Just because you've done something 'silly' or 'mean' doesn't make you a 'silly' or 'mean' person.

Old 'evidence': Specific problems you've experienced

Even self-confident people know that they're not perfect, that they have shortcomings, some of which they would like to change or improve. But people who lack self-confidence see these shortcomings as evidence that they're somehow basically faulty, instead of as specific problems to overcome. When Kevin was struggling to fill in a complicated mortgage application form, he saw this as further evidence of his stupidity, when in fact the form would have been hard-going even for someone who hadn't got dyslexia.

Reassess it: Are you using double standards – would you condemn or blame a friend who was having the same problem in the same way? So why are you convinced that the difficulties you face are 'evidence' of everything that's wrong with you? So you're forgetful, you're always late, you can't do small-talk – is this really evidence that your Bottom Line is spot-on? It's normal and human to be aware of something about yourself that you would like to improve! Taking a more tolerant approach to yourself can help you move forward and turn down the volume on the critical inner voice that holds you back.

Old 'evidence': The way you look

If you could 'Photoshop' your body, which bits would you change? Would you get rid of that cellulite, or give yourself a six-pack? Shrink your nose, smooth your complexion or straighten your teeth? Who hasn't got a 'makeover' wish-list? But if you lack self-confidence, it might go beyond day-dreaming – are you fixated on a body part and convinced you will never be happy or 100 per cent accept-able as a person while it's there? Nicki's whole self-image depended on being below a certain weight (her 'acceptable' weight). If the scale showed less than 70kg, she felt OK. But if it nudged above this mark, her mood would plum-met. She'd immediately feel like an unattractive person that no one would want around. Even if she'd felt good about herself the day before, she now had evidence that she was fat and ugly.

Reassess it: People stand on a range of different boxes to boost their self-confidence. When you can't get on your box, you're left feeling at the mercy of those nega-tive beliefs about yourself. It may not be your appearance – work is another common one. If your career is one of the boxes you rely on to stand tall, it's hard not to take redundancy personally and as a sign that you're not good enough. Relying for your self-confidence on things that are not completely under your control inevitably makes you vulnerable to low self-confidence – you're left standing, and you've got the 'evidence' to prove your Bottom Line. If your self-confidence depends on your looks, simply getting older is likely to support your Bottom Line that you're inferior, or not attractive. Or if feeling good about yourself depends completely on being a good mother, you'll find it hard not to feel worthless when your children leave home.

To reassess this evidence, take another look at your list of positive qualities (page 122). Do a lot of the qualities, strengths, skills and talents on your list depend on the thing you're basing your self-confidence on? Think about some people you like and respect (people you know in real life, not celebrities) and write down the things you value in them – perhaps their courage, their cheerfulness, their ability to stay calm under pressure. Now, considering the reasons you value each of these other people, how important is the one reason behind your own self-confidence or lack of confidence? How important is it that your wardrobe is full of fashionable clothes, or that you stay slim, or your house always looks elegant?

Nicki's self-confidence was based on her weight. But when she listed her positive qualities (her sense of humour, enthusiasm for life, her interest in and compassion for other people, her talent for cooking, her ability to think laterally at work and come up with solutions to problems), she could see that these were the real evidence of who she was, not what it said on the scales! She also made a list of people she liked and respected and wrote down what she saw as attractive in each one. Being thin and fit hardly featured – the qualities that came at the top were sense of humour, reliability, and common sense. Doing this exercise was the start of a major shift for Nicki in truly accepting herself for who she was, rather than judging herself by a quality that she simply thought she should have (a weight of under 70kg).

Old 'evidence': Individual differences

However funny, attractive or intelligent you are, if you look for them you'll find other people who are funnier, more attractive, more intelligent. People who lack self-confidence have a tendency to compare themselves to other people, and use what they find as 'evidence' to support their Bottom Line. Paul, for example, was always comparing his own social life with what he heard people talking about at work, and he inevitably felt he didn't have much of a life. Rather than judging his life as unique to him, he used negative comparisons to fuel the sense that he was unlovable.

Reassess it: Just because someone else excels at something, does that mean you're no good at it? There will always be someone who has a bigger house, a more prestigious job, a more conventionally attractive physical appearance, or a more stable family life. But no one excels at everything. Try comparing a rugby player with a ballet dancer with a paramedic – could you say who was fitter, more skilled, more talented? Can you stand back and see differences between yourself and other people as just that – differences

– rather than evidence of your own shortcomings as a person?

Old 'evidence': Other people's behaviour

You already know that the way you were treated as a child by the people around you – family, friends and society in general – played a pivotal role in establishing your Bottom Line. And if you've grown up with the 'evidence' that being treated badly means you're a bad person, or that you must have 'asked for it', any bad treatment you encounter as an adult will also be added to your evidence collection. A surly sales assistant, a moody work colleague, an inconsiderate partner, an unreliable friend – it all becomes evidence that you're no good, and you deserve it.

Reassess it: If your self-confidence is low and other people treat you badly or react to you negatively, your instinct is to think you deserve it or have provoked it in some way. But think about that logically. So that means you're assuming that the rude, aggressive or bad-tempered person you encountered is an angel the rest of the time, and treats every other human being with courtesy and respect? Or if (in the case of a partner, for example) they *do* seem to treat everyone else better than they treat you, could this be *their* problem, not yours? Pinning your self-worth on other people's moods and behaviour towards you is like pinning it on the weather – you have about the same level of control! It's also illogical – if on the same afternoon one person treats you well (boosting your self-confidence) but then another person snubs you (sending it crashing), what does it say about you: are you OK, or not OK?

If your Bottom Line includes being unlikable or not worthy of approval, then you'll never be short of evidence to back it up, because no one can be universally liked or approved of the whole time. Be honest, do *you* like every single person you meet? So why expect everyone to like you? Some people click, some don't – it's a quirk of human nature. To please everyone, you'd have to become a human chameleon.

If there's one particular person you come into contact with on a regular basis and who seems to confirm your deepest negative beliefs about yourself, think of why might that be, apart from any individual feelings they might have towards you. It's not easy to take a step back if the person is someone close to you, like your partner or a parent, or someone in authority, such as a tutor, boss or manager. But can you at least consider the possibility that they'd behave badly whether or not you were in their life? Are they critical or dismissive of *everyone,* not just you? Maybe their default mood is cynicism or distrust. Or they could be under stress, or have a condition that affects them psychologically, or problems with alcohol or drug misuse.

Old 'evidence': The behaviour of your children

Your eight-year-old is sent home from school for hitting other children and your first thought is 'It's my fault! I don't give him enough attention!' Or your thirteen-year-old comes home drunk from a party, and what do you think – 'I should have seen the signs!' Your sixteen-year-old daughter develops an eating disorder – do you agonise over where you went wrong? Being a parent is never easy but if you lack self-confidence it's hard not to blame yourself when a child seems to be going off the rails. It's easy to use their behaviour as evidence to support your Bottom Line – that you're somehow inferior to everyone else, or you're no good at anything you do, or you're bound to fail.

Reassess it: Parenthood offers no end of opportunities for guilt and self-recrimination. It's impossible to be a perfect parent at all times – it's probably never been done. But even if by some miracle or fluke of nature, you did manage to be the world's very first perfect parent, chances are, you still wouldn't produce a perfect child! It's simply not possible to control the emotions, actions and behaviour of another human being in this way. After all, once a child reaches a certain age, you're no longer with them every hour of every day. As they get older, other influences such as friends, teachers and images from the media compete for attention. Depending for your self-worth on a child's behaviour not only sets you up to fail, it's also not great for your child. It's hard not to over-react to problems when your own self-esteem is at stake, so it creates its own vicious circle – your anger or disappointment can trigger *more* difficult behaviour. Being a responsible parent, setting boundaries and being consistent, being open, supportive, available and loving towards a child – these are all good reasons to feel good about yourself. But it is *not* reasonable to base your self-confidence on whether your child does well at school, never gets into trouble, and chooses a 'good' career path!

Step 2: Collect new evidence

So, now you know your old evidence was pretty unreliable, you need to find some alternatives. You can start to amass 'good evidence' even if you haven't finalised your 'New

Bottom Line'. The new evidence can help to undermine your Old Bottom Line, and could also help crystallise your New Bottom Line in your mind.

Remember the 'thinking filters' from Chapter 2, how biases in the way you see the world around you can mean you focus on information that supports the Bottom Line, and screen out or dismiss information which contradicts it? Now, it's time to do the opposite, and actively seek out and record information which directly *contradicts* your Old Bottom Line, and supports a more realistic, positive view of yourself.

First, work out exactly what you're looking for. This will depend on your Old Bottom Line. If, for example, your Old Bottom Line is 'I am an outsider' and your New Bottom Line is 'I am acceptable', then what you're looking for is evidence that proves that you're acceptable (being voted on to a committee, invited to social events, asked for your opinion and advice). Or if your Old Bottom Line was 'I am unlovable' and your New Bottom Line is 'I am likable', then you need to collect the evidence for your likability (getting lots of cards on your birthday, getting a hug from a friend, your three-year-old telling you she loves you).

You're looking for evidence that not only contradicts your Old Bottom Line, illustrating that it's out of date, unfair or just wrong, *but also* supports your New Bottom Line as being realistic and believable. To give you an idea of the kind of things you're looking for, have a look at the next panel, which shows what the people you met in Chapter 2 came up with when they did this exercise.

NEW BOTTOM LINE EVIDENCE

	Old Bottom Line	New Bottom Line	Supporting evidence for NBL
Charlotte	I am a joke	I am who I am and that's OK	Things I have achieved (my designs) My work – doing well in a competitive arena My motivation – putting effort into healthy eating and keeping fit My relationships – having good friends who make an effort to include me in their life My good points
Kevin	I am stupid	I am adaptable	The way I have got on in life despite having dyslexia My ability to make the best of every situation My talent for creating a good atmosphere among the people I work with

Nicki	I am fat and ugly	I am attractive just as I am	All the good qualities I have that are nothing to do with physical appearance (from my list – note daily examples)
			My happy marriage to a man who tells me he finds me attractive
			People responding warmly to me (smiling, laughing at my jokes, people sitting next to me, looking pleased to see me)
Anna	I am unimportant	I am important	My positive qualities (keep recording examples)
			The good things in my life that I deserve (my new flat, my friends, my job)
			My passion for music and motivation to get better at playing the piano
			My courage to end an unhealthy relationship

Paul	I am unlovable	I am lovable	My good friends and the things they do that show they care for me (organising a birthday party, ringing me, asking me to go on holiday with them)
			The good things in me that mean I am a lovable person (my loyalty, my thoughtfulness, my willingness to act responsibly)
Meena	I am inferior I am a misfit	I am worthy I belong	My group of friends who are always there for me
			My ability to put people at their ease
			My boss's support and positive reaction when I told him I was being given too much work
			My list of good points

Jackson	I am not good enough	I am good enough	Positive responses when I dare to be myself and give my energy full rein (people joining in, being fired by my enthusiasm)
			People laughing at my funny stories at parties
			Winning my last contract despite putting a limit on the hours I spent working on it
			The love of my wife, children and good friends
			My parents finally telling me that they are very proud of me
Carol	I am incompetent	I am competent	My glowing reference from my former boss, and my years of good service
			Colleagues recommending me for new jobs
			Getting accepted on a course to retrain as a counsellor and put my experience to use helping others

Step 3: Test out your theories

It's time for experimenting again! If you've got a good idea of your New Bottom Line, it's tempting to think all the hard work is done. It's true that you've come a long way, but giving up now would be like dropping out of a marathon just as the finishing line came into view. To make sure your New Bottom Line becomes part of your unconscious, influencing the way you think, act and feel, you need to get some positive experiences in the bank to draw on. Now is the time to push back the walls of the prison that low self-confidence has built around you, by experimenting with acting as if your New Bottom Line were true.

If you set up and carried out experiments to test out the validity of anxious predictions, experiments to act against self-critical thoughts, and some to test-drive new Rules for Living, you know what to expect. But don't worry if you feel uncomfortable or even fearful at the thought of doing this. Don't panic or use it as an excuse to put the book down and do something else. Instead, try to calmly notice what thoughts run through your mind when you imagine acting differently, trying out new situations, or being your true self around people. Chances are, you will find anxious predictions and self-critical thoughts lurking behind these feelings. If so, come up with more realistic alternatives to your predictions, and to your self-critical thoughts, before you start your experiment.

How do you decide what experiments to do? Look for experiences that would support your new perspective on yourself. You may get ideas from the situations you found yourself avoiding when you were working on anxious predictions. Or maybe you can take inspiration from the work you did on self-acceptance and building rewards and pleasure into your life. How could that work help you identify the right kind of experiences now? Here are examples of experiments carried out by the people from Chapter 2.

EXPERIMENTS FOR MY NEW BOTTOM LINE

	New Bottom Line	Experiments
Charlotte	I am who I am and that's OK	Ask my parents to come to the next fashion show of my new season designs Plan more treats and pleasures for myself Sign up for that evening class in life drawing
Kevin	I am adaptable	Look into local adult education courses on overcoming dyslexia Tell people about the problem instead of trying to pretend it doesn't exist Talk to my boss about the possibility of promotion
Nicki	I am attractive just as I am	Stop weighing myself every morning Go shopping and choose clothes that I actually like, rather than things that cover me up and that I think will draw attention away from size Get up and dance at the wedding we're going to next month, instead of watching from the sidelines
Anna	I am important	Ask people for help at work when I need it When people ask me how I am, stop pretending I'm always 'fine' and start acting as if I am entitled

		to people's time and attention by being open with them
		Ask a group of friends to join me at my favourite restaurant for my birthday next month
Paul	I am lovable	Ask Helen if she'd like to go out to dinner with me, then tell her how much I like her
		Be more open about my past
		Make the first approach to people I trust, rather than waiting for them to come to me
Meena	I am worthy I belong	Speak up in meetings, expressing my own ideas before people hijack them. Write them down and present them as proposals to my boss.
		Tell my boss when she's overloading me with work
		Spend at least an hour an day doing something relaxing and pleasurable
Jackson	I am good enough	Spend less time preparing assignments and documents
		Leave the office by 6.30 every day
		Say, 'I don't know,' when I can't answer a question
Carol	I am competent	Talk to an employment lawyer about a claim for unfair dismissal
		Update my CV and start applying for jobs

Alternatively, visualise a person with your New Bottom Line and think about how they would act on a daily basis, in their work, social life and close relationships. Could you try out any of these things as mini-experiments in your daily life?

Step 4: Pull it all together

Add your ideas to your **Updating my Bottom Line worksheet**. To get the best out of your experiments, review them and write down how they went. This helps them become firm 'evidence' in your mind, part of your new collection of experiences that confirm your New Bottom Line. When your new way of behaving goes well, put it in your Positives notebook so you can re-read about it when you need a boost.

UPDATING MY BOTTOM LINE WORKSHEET

My Old Bottom Line:

	Belief	Emotions (0 to 10)
When the Old Bottom Line is most convincing:	____%	_____
When it is least convincing:	____%	_____
When I started the book:	____%	_____

My New Bottom Line:

	Belief	Emotions (0 to 10)
When the New Bottom Line is most convincing:	____%	_____
When it is least convincing:	____%	_____
When I started the book:	____%	_____

'Evidence' for my Old Bottom Line and my new understanding

'Evidence'   *New understanding*

In the light of this new understanding, I now believe my
   Old Bottom Line: ____%

In the light of this new understanding, I now believe my
   New Bottom Line: ____%

Evidence (past and present) that supports my New Bottom Line

In the light of this evidence, I now believe my
Old Bottom Line: ____%

In the light of this evidence, I now believe my
New Bottom Line: ____%

Things to notice as evidence for my New Bottom Line

Testing it out

MEENA'S UPDATING MY BOTTOM LINE WORKSHEET

My Old Bottom Line: I am inferior / I am a misfit

	Belief	*Emotions* (0 to 10)
When the Old Bottom Line is most convincing:	95%	Anxiety **9** Despair **9**
When it is least convincing:	30%	Anxiety **4** Despair **3**
When I started the book:	75%	Anxiety **7.5** Despair **6**

My New Bottom Line: I am worthy / I belong

	Belief	*Emotions* (0 to 10)
When the New Bottom Line is most convincing:	50%	Confidence **7.5** Contentment **6**
When it is least convincing:	30%	Confidence **1** Contentment **1**
When I started the book:	0%	Confidence **0** Contentment **0**

'Evidence' for my Old Bottom Line and my new understanding

'Evidence'	*New understanding*
I never fitted in at school	I was shy and my parents' attitude that the people at school weren't 'our sort' didn't help. Nor did the way the girls reacted to me when I spoke up
Not getting promoted in my job	The right promotion for me hasn't come up yet
	The people who were promoted ahead of me were doing different jobs

| | Until now, I haven't felt confident enough to present myself in the best light – I'm already changing that |
| My first serious boyfriend dumping me | He has also dumped every other girl he's been with since and never stays with someone for very long |

In the light of this new understanding, I now believe my
  Old Bottom Line: **30%**

In the light of this new understanding, I now believe my
  New Bottom Line: **75%**

Evidence (past and present) that supports my New Bottom Line

My parents loved me and did all they could to give me a good life, but they had their own self-confidence issues which they passed on to me

I wasn't in with the 'cool crowd' at school but I made some good friends that I'm still in touch with today

I got a job with a good PR agency and I know my boss really values and relies on me

I was approached by a headhunter for a job at another agency last year

I have lots of good friends who really care about me

My best friend told me that I'm a great dinner party guest because I put everyone at their ease and get everyone talking

In the light of this evidence, I now believe my
  Old Bottom Line: **20%**

In the light of this evidence, I now believe my
  New Bottom Line: **85%**

Things to notice as evidence for my New Bottom Line

People I care about ringing, texting and emailing me as if they really want to keep in touch

New people I meet being interested in what I have to say and suggesting we meet again

My boss taking notice of my point of view at work

Testing it out

Be more assertive at work when I feel I'm being overloaded or people are taking credit for my ideas

Have the courage to say what I think and observe the outcome

Plan more treats and pleasures for myself

Join a local running club and meet men who share my interest in exercise and the outdoors

Talk to my boss about my opportunities for promotion

- Don't expect overnight miracles. If your Old Bottom Line has been in place for some time, it will take time, patience and practice to make the new one powerfully convincing. It may take some time before you feel fully convinced by your New Bottom Line. But changing your behaviour, even in little ways, so that you act as if you do believe it will help make it happen.
- You need a clear-out! Throw away that dark, depressing, self-defeating, confidence-crushing evidence that you used in support of the Old Bottom Line – you don't need it any more. Replace it with some uplifting, mood-boosting positive evidence that supports your image of yourself, and helps your self-confidence grow.

ESSENTIAL TAKE-HOME MESSAGES FROM THIS CHAPTER

- Building self-confidence isn't about creating an inflated image for yourself ('I'm actually almost perfect!'). The exercises in this book aren't about the power of positive thinking – you don't have to tell yourself that 'every day in every way, you are getting better and better'! They are about truth, honesty and integrity. They are about living in the real world. Being self-confident doesn't mean glossing over your weaknesses and flaws or pretending there's no room for improvement, or you have nothing left to learn. It means having a realistic, balanced, un-skewed view of yourself, of your weaknesses and flaws, and of your strengths and good qualities.

Life Lesson

If you were always lovable, always competent, always worthy, always intelligent or always attractive, you'd be the only member of the human race to achieve that peak of perfection.

9

SHAPE YOUR FUTURE

As you near the end of this book, you may already feel that big shifts are happening in your life. Right now, the insights you've gained about yourself are shining brightly in your awareness and you may feel that you will never go back to your old way of thinking. But these insights and this new awareness can fade away after you close this book and get on with day-to-day living. Alternatively, you may feel that you've learned a lot, but that the new ways of thinking and acting towards yourself are still insubstantial. This is especially likely to be true if you've lacked confidence for many years and that has played a big role in shaping your life.

In this final chapter you will learn . . .

- How to write a Self-Confidence Protection Plan. This will help consolidate what you have learnt from this book and to ensure your New Bottom Line is at the heart of your thoughts, feelings and behaviour in the future.
- What to do if you experience a set-back.

But first, let's take a quick overview of how all the changes you've made so far fit together.

HOW THE JIGSAW FITS TOGETHER

You've done a lot of work since you first picked up this book! You've looked into where your lack of self-confidence came from, questioned your negative thinking habits, pushed the boundaries and carried out experiments, tried out some new Rules for Living and come up with a New Bottom Line. But how does it all fit together? Perhaps it's easiest to describe with a flow chart.

My Journey to Confidence

What experiences (relationships or events) sowed the seeds of my negative self-image?

What helped that negative self-image grow and kept it going?

What 'evidence' supported my low opinion of myself?

Changing My Rules for Living

What were my old Rules for Living? How did they work *against* me?

What Rules would work *for* me?

How did I try them out?

Identifying my Old Bottom Line

What were my deepest, core negative beliefs about myself?

What 'evidence' made me believe them?

What's my new view of this 'evidence'?

↓

Creating a New Bottom Line

What is my New Bottom Line – my updated, more realistic and helpful self-image?

What evidence *supports* my New Bottom Line and *contradicts* the old one?

What changes have I made that shows my New Bottom Line works for me?

THE END OF THE VICIOUS CIRCLE!

There's no way you can guarantee that you'll never have another bad thought about yourself again. Certain situations or people could make the shadows of your Old Bottom Line spring up. But the difference is that you've put in place several effective 'stops' that will prevent low mood or anxious thoughts from triggering the old vicious circle of low self-confidence.

Certain feelings, thoughts and behaviours create echoes of your old Bottom Line, leading to:

↓	↓	↓
Negative predictions	**Unhelpful behaviour**	**Self-critical thoughts**
Stop it! Identify, question and test with experiments	Stop it! Face things you avoid, drop unnecessary precautions, focus on your successes	Stop it! Identify and question. Encourage and praise yourself, and treat yourself like someone who deserves

the good things
in life.

Recognise your
good points and
give yourself
credit for your
achievements

↓

**Result: Anxiety and depression are nipped in the bud, and
your Old Bottom Line is weakened, not strengthened.**

DO SOME RISK-PREVENTION

When you are under stress, or feeling low, unwell or tired,
you may feel echoes of your Old Bottom Line creeping
into your thinking. The odd critical comment might flash
through your mind, or you might find your thinking turns
generally negative, and focuses on what's going wrong, and
what's gone wrong in the past. Your behaviour will subtly
start to change – depending on your Old Bottom Line, you
might put more pressure on yourself to work harder, or
start to withdraw socially, or go back to weighing yourself
every day. You might stop making time for relaxation or
fun. You tell yourself you're just 'busy', but your mood has
also taken a dip – along with your confidence.

First of all, be reassured that this is normal and, because
you now know how to break the vicious circle that keeps
low self-confidence going, it isn't anything to panic about.
You need to be realistic and accept that it's highly likely
a setback will happen at some point. Being aware of the
early warning signs that your old self-image is returning
will help you hold up the Stop! sign to your Old Bottom
Line as early as possible, before it's had time to run you

down. Eventually, you'll get to the point where you can simply think, 'I don't need this back in my life, it does nothing positive for me.' But right now, it may take a little more effort.

Coming up against challenges isn't always a bad thing – you'll probably learn something every time your confidence takes a temporary dip which could help to add depth and dimension to your new healthy, accepting self-image. But a bit of forward-planning is a good idea – by anticipating your 'at-risk' situations, you can minimise the emotional upheaval and disruption in your life. One way to do this is to create a Self-Confidence Protection Plan that consolidates your new way of thinking, but also prepares for setbacks.

✏ TIME TO GET WRITING:

Your Self-Confidence Protection Plan

Your Self-Confidence Protection Plan will be a two-page document that answers seven crucial questions (see *Time to get writing: Answering your seven crucial questions* on pages 228–9). It's almost like a crib sheet of everything you've learned in this book, in an easy-to-read format. Ideas and insights can fade from consciousness – even if you really believe them. Your Self-Confidence Protection Plan is a way of reinforcing them, while you go about your everyday life. But it's most powerful if you really get it right.

How to do it

Draft 1: Answer the seven crucial questions on a piece of paper, in as much detail as you can. This is the first draft of your Self-Confidence Protection Plan. Read through to see if you've left anything important out – have another look at the notes you've made while working through this book, particularly your worksheets and Positives Notebook. Then carry out your draft Plan for 14 to 21 days. At the end of that period, make time to review it.

- **Write down the date and time of your review in your diary or on your calendar *right now*. Don't put it off or you may forget to do it. This is something you are doing for yourself. It's important – and you deserve it.**

Draft 2: Review the success of your first draft. How helpful is your Plan? How did it work when you put it into practice? Were there bits that didn't translate to real life? Or was there something missing that would have been helpful? Write out a revised version – this is draft 2. Put a review date in your diary for at least three months ahead. Now, put draft 2 into practice for a minimum of three months.

Draft 3: When the second test period is up, it's time for a final review. How helpful has your Plan proved to be over this longer test period? Did you feel it gave you the support you need? What difference has it made to your self-confidence – has it consolidated your good work? Do you feel your self-confidence has grown or developed in any way? Did your Plan help you to deal with setbacks effectively, or do you need another contingency plan? What other changes do you want to make?

Tips for making this work

- Drafting and test-running may seem like a bit of a hassle. You may be tempted to skip the reviews – or convinced you can get it right first time. If you really can't face the review process, then go with your first draft – it's better than not having a Self-Confidence Protection Plan at all. Or maybe commit to doing one review – if it goes well, your second draft may be your final draft. But if you find yourself slipping into old habits in the future, there's a good chance your Plan still has some holes and could use a review. So make whatever changes are necessary, and test out your new version for a limited period that you agree with yourself. Then review and rewrite.

- Prepare for change. Bear in mind that unless you have a very accurate crystal ball, your Self-Confidence Protection Plan will never anticipate every setback or change in your circumstances! So in theory, you could keep redrafting. However helpful it is now, your Plan may feel out of date as your life moves on. Be prepared to tweak it at any future point to take account of new roles you take on, or new relationships. The best Self-Confidence Protection Plans are flexible.

- Make a big deal about your reviews! Treat yourself to lunch at your favourite cafe or restaurant, or find a peaceful space in your house, where you can have some time to yourself without interruptions.

- Be SMART. Before you start answering your seven crucial questions, take a tip from the business world, and keep the SMART rules in the back of your mind as you write your Plan:

  S Is it **Simple** and **Specific** enough? Is your Plan no more than two pages long?

  M Is it **Measurable**? How can you measure whether you've achieved what you planned? Write down how you expect, or hope, to be feeling after carrying out your Plan for six months. What will your daily life look like? What will you be doing that you're not doing now?

A Is it **Agreed**? Have you thought about how your Plan will affect the people around you (see below for more on this)? Do you have their support?

R Is it **Realistic**? Does your Plan take into account your time, finances, physical and emotional health, and the level of support from friends, family and colleagues?

T Is the **Timescale** reasonable? How much time each day will you need to put your plan into practice? How long do you need between reviews to assess whether it's working?

HOW CHANGES IN YOU AFFECT THOSE AROUND YOU

Changes in you inevitably affect those closest to you. Because your changes are positive and life-enhancing, the ripple effect means the lives of those around will ultimately benefit, too. But there may be an initial adjustment period while people get used to the 'new' you. Changes such as being more vocal about your feelings, or more assertive in general, can be disconcerting for people, and even frightening – especially if they're not expecting them, or don't understand why you've changed. So try to involve those closest to you so they know what to expect. Perhaps you could explain that you're working on your self-confidence, and ask them for their help and patience?

If you've decided that you need to give yourself more time to do the things that you enjoy, and to do that you need more help with domestic tasks, you need to explain to the family why it's important that you make these changes, and give them specific tasks. You should also factor in the fact that they may be reluctant at first to follow your suggestions, and that you may have to tell them what you want to happen a few times before it sinks in.

But even if you don't wish to directly involve others, it's worth considering the impact that changes in you will have on the people around you. Are they likely to act negatively in any way? What do you predict? And how might you deal with negative reactions?

✏ TIME TO GET WRITING:

Answering your seven crucial questions

The answers to these questions will form your Self-Confidence Protection Plan. Here they are, with explanations below. You'll get the idea from Paul's plan a few pages further on.

1 What stopped my self-confidence from developing?

2 What kept it down?

3 What have I learned from working through the book?

4 What did I discover were my most important unhelpful thoughts, Rules and beliefs? What alternatives did I find to them?

5 How can I help my self-confidence grow in the future?

6 What are my danger zones?

7 If I face a setback, what will I do about it?

Q 1 What stopped my self-confidence from developing?

Look again at the 'back story' you wrote for Chapter 7 (page 168). If you can think of other appropriate things to include, rewrite it now. Include brief summaries of the events, experiences and relationships that stopped your self-confidence from developing naturally and that put, or kept, your Old Bottom Line in place.

Q 2 What kept it down?

What unhelpful Rules for Living did you develop to cope with your Bottom Line, and make yourself feel acceptable? How did your thinking style undermine your confidence – what were your self-critical thoughts and anxious predictions? What positive things about you and your life did you dismiss or ignore? What self-defeating behaviour stopped you from pushing your boundaries, and learning that your anxious predictions were unrealistic?

Q 3 What have I learned from working through the book?

Review the work you've done and pull out the highlights for you – the ideas that really hit home. Which exercises were the most productive? What insights were the most revealing? What new habits have you learned?

Q 4 What did I discover were my most important unhelpful thoughts, Rules and beliefs? What alternatives did I find to them?

Draw a vertical line down the centre of the page and head the left-hand side 'Unhelpful Thoughts' and the other 'Positive Alternatives'. In the left-hand column, list your anxious predictions, self-critical thoughts, unhelpful Rules for Living and Old Bottom Line. In the right-hand column, come up with a succinct, more helpful alternative to each one.

Q 5 How can I help my self-confidence grow in the future?

What do you need to do to build on your hard work, to allow for more insights, understanding and learning in the future? What do you still need to work on to fully develop your self-confidence? Do you need to learn more about the way you relate to the world around you? Do you need to go back to particular parts of the book and work through some sections again? Or maybe you're inspired to do some further reading, or curious to try some one-on-one CBT? Here are some more ideas to mull over:

- Are there fuzzy bits in your understanding of how your low self-confidence developed and what kept it going? If so, how could you go about exploring them?
- Do any particular situations still make you feel anxious, but you're not sure why? How can you find out what's going on under the surface? Be honest – are there situations that you still approach with self-protective precautions in place? How can you go about giving up those precautions? There's a very good chance you're going to face situations that make you anxious in the future – how will you deal with them?
- How will you keep your mental radar tuned to spot self-critical thoughts before they take hold? What might be the first signs that your old habits are creeping back in?
- Will you keep patting yourself on the back and acknowledging your positive qualities, your skills,

your strengths and talents, even when life gets busy? Do you need to keep up your Positives Notebook to make sure? Or on days when you don't have time to fill it in, at least look over some past pages?

- Will you find it easy to keep a daily balance of 'A' activities (your achievements, including ordinary tasks, chores, obligations) and 'P' activities (pleasure and relaxation)? (Have another look at your Positives Notebook.) If it gets more difficult when you're under stress, would a few days of forward-planning help?

- How convincing do you now find your Rules for Living? If you're still not sure your new Rules are good ones, or have some difficulty making them work for you, what do you need to do to believe in them so that it feels natural to act on them? Will re-reading your **Changing the Rules worksheet** help?

- How can you strengthen your belief in your New Bottom Line? How can you protect it when you're feeling unhappy or under pressure? What little clues about yourself do you need to tune into every day, and mentally take note of? Would re-reading your **Updating my Bottom Line worksheet** help? What mini-experiments can you weave into your daily life to ensure you keep pushing the boundaries?

Q 6 What are my danger zones?

Can you envisage any situations in the future that might bring back your old feelings or low self-confidence? The notes that you made when you worked on Chapter 3, about what has activated your Old Bottom Line in the past, will be helpful here. What are your personal danger zones, the areas of your life where you're the most vulnerable? Some

common danger zones are personal illness, relationship difficulties, money problems, and spending time with a particular
family member who knocks your self-image. Forewarned is
forearmed – you might not be able to completely prevent the
old feelings, but you can make sure you're ready for them,
so you don't over-react or let them take hold.

Q 7 If I face a setback, what will I do about it?

First, don't ignore the signals from your early warning
system! It's tempting to carry on and act as if nothing is
happening, but this is the point at which you need to stop,
think and make some changes. When your stress levels go
up, or your self-critical thinking creeps in, or your old habits reappear, you need to find out what's really happening.
Ask yourself, why have I skipped my afternoon walk three
days in a row – is it *really* because I'm extra busy, or is
it because I've stopped prioritising looking after myself?
And why have I done that – did that cutting remark about
my weight from my mother last week actually hit home?
Or if you had a disagreement with your partner and took
the path of least resistance, keeping quiet about your real
feelings and putting up with behaviour you knew wasn't
right, ask yourself, what's made me think my needs aren't
important? Are the shadows of my old self-image, my Old
Bottom Line, creeping back in? If you suspect this might be
happening, act now rather than later. Every second counts.

WHAT TO DO IF YOU EXPERIENCE A SETBACK

If you notice early warning signals that your Old Bottom
Line is coming to life again, what should you do?

- **Keep calm!** You're on an incredible journey and there are bound to be rocky bits, pauses and obstacles along the way. But as long as you keep going in the right direction, you'll be OK. Try to keep a sense of perspective. You've come a long way and you'll never completely go back to the way you were. Something has shifted inside you and it's made big changes. But you need to nurture your new perspective on the world and protect it from old habits, especially at vulnerable times. That means acting sooner, rather than later. So if you've had an upsetting experience at work, find a quiet space and re-read your Positives Notebook for ten minutes. Had an argument with a friend or partner? Take a break, and as you release it, allow your body to relax. Then re-read your list of good qualities. Use your imagination to bring each one to life.

- **Re-do the exercises.** If you've gone into anxious prediction mode, start to fill out the **Anxious predictions worksheet** again. Work out exactly what you're predicting, come up with a more realistic alternative, and find a way of doing a mini-experiment to test it out. Feeling guilty about taking time out just for you, or feeling your life isn't really going anywhere? Start filling out the Daily Activity Diary again, and making sure every day includes things that give you pleasure, and things that give you a sense of achievement. It's not a backward step, it's consolidating what you've learned so far.

- **Take it further.** If you find you're having setback after setback, consider one-to-one therapy. You haven't failed if you've worked through this book and still feel you need professional help. If you liked the ideas in this book, and think they work for you, then a cognitive behavior therapist could help you take things further.

Paul's Self-Confidence Protection Plan

This is the Plan that Paul came up with.

1 What stopped my self-confidence from developing?

My mother had trouble bonding with me when I was born. I was in an incubator for several weeks and my parents expected me to die. When I came home, my mother was terrified that I would die. She suffered from post-natal depression and couldn't cope with my crying or problems with feeding. She was very young, and spent hours on her own with me, while dad was at work. As I got older, my parents started to grow apart as my dad spent more and more evenings out at the pub. That put further stress on my mother. She was given medication from her doctor that made her feel disconnected from life, so she spent most of my childhood in a daze. She wasn't well enough to give me the attention and love that a child needs, but I grew up thinking it was my fault, and that I was unlovable. This was my Old Bottom Line. Once this idea was in place, other things happened that seemed to confirm it. My grandmother, who I had been very close to and who was almost like a mother to me, died when I was ten. My parents divorced soon after and my dad made no effort to keep in touch with me. My mother's mental health improved and she remarried and had two more children, but seeing her giving them the physical affection and care and attention she couldn't give me just confirmed that it was my fault and I was unlovable.

2 What kept it down?

I lived my life as if I really was an unlovable person. I put a wall up between me and other people. As a child, I withdrew into my shell, and spent hours on my own in my room reading books. I never asked for help from other people or told them about my feelings. I was always good at fixing things, and got the hang of new technology, and that meant I could fit in and be part of the gang. But I never let friends get close to me – I thought that if they did, they would realise I was unlovable. When my friends started to ask girls out on dates, I pretended I wasn't interested as I thought I would only be rejected. I stayed in and studied rather than go to discos and parties with my friends. I made friends at university, and did a fair amount of the usual drinking and partying. But whenever a girl seemed interested in getting close to me, I put up barriers and pushed her away so she didn't get a chance to see how unlovable I was.

3 What have I learned from working through the book?

That my Old Bottom Line was understandable, given my experiences as a child, and my lack of love from both my mother and my father. But the fact that it happened to me doesn't mean that I deserved it, or caused it in any way. It was just bad luck, the consequence of a series of unfortunate events. To survive, I created Rules to live by to protect myself and make myself more acceptable. But I have learned that my Rules are holding me back from living the life I really want for myself – a loving relationship and one day a family of my own. By focusing on the good things about me, and by checking out my anxious predictions, I can change the way I think.

4 What did I discover were my most important unhelpful thoughts, Rules and beliefs? What alternatives did I find to them?

I am unlovable	→	I am lovable
If I let anyone get close to me, they will see how unlovable I am and reject me	→	If I let people get close to me, I get the warmth and affection I need. Most people will treat me decently, and I can protect myself from those who don't
If I ask for what I need, I will be disappointed	→	Asking people for help makes them feel needed by me and brings me closer to them. People who care about me will try their best to give me what I ask for

5 How can I help my self-confidence grow in the future?

Keep reading the worksheets for my new Rules and New Bottom Line so I can really drum in what I have learned. Keep acting *as if* they were true and see what difference it makes. When I can feel myself getting anxious and putting up my protective wall, try to work out what I'm worried might happen. Take a step back, assess how likely this is, and look for an alternative perspective. I need to watch out for self-criticism – it's an old habit and I need to nip it in the bud before it starts. Keep up my Positives Notebook – it only takes a few minutes and it really works for me. Be more open with women, let them get close to me and put more effort into getting to know the ones I really like.

6 What are my danger zones?

Being rejected by a woman I really like and who I have got close to, or worrying that rejection is likely. Falling out with a good friend.

7 If I face a setback, what will I do about it?

Be aware of the early warning signs – watch out for self-criticism and anxious predictions. Watch out for protective behaviour – am I starting to withdraw, to push someone away? Be open with the person in question and explain how I am feeling. Re-read the notes I've made throughout this book, especially the worksheets and this Self-Confidence Protection Plan, remind myself how far I've come, and maybe do an exercise again. If I take a risk and get close to a woman but the relationship doesn't work out, don't assume it's because I'm unlovable – look for more realistic alternative explanations. Be more compassionate towards myself and if I find I keep getting into difficulties, invest in some counselling sessions to reinforce and build on the work I've done so far.

ESSENTIAL TAKE-HOME MESSAGES FROM THIS CHAPTER

- **Changes in you mean changes for other people.** Getting those closest to you on board by asking for their help and support can help make the transition to your new way of living go as smoothly as possible. If that's not possible, then keep them in the loop – explain what you're doing and how it might change the way you behave. But remember, you don't need their permission or approval to do this. The only approval you need comes from within.

- **You need a Self-Confidence Protection Plan.** We know you have a busy life, and you can't devote all your time to your 'self-confidence boosting' project. But can you work out a way to fit some essential maintenance into your everyday life? Remember, how you feel about yourself affects everything – your relationships, your career, and your motivation to be healthy. It doesn't have to be complicated – answering the seven crucial questions will help you come up with a strategy that works for you.

- **If your don't use your Plan, you'll lose it!** So don't file it away and forget it, or leave it lying around getting tattered and marked (that's like telling yourself that it's not important). Put it in a protective plastic sleeve or in an envelope and store it somewhere it will be safe and private, but where you can get it easily, such as your desk drawer or bedside table.

- **Expect setbacks.** Right now, you're probably feeling that you'll never go back to your old ways. You're revelling in your new self-confidence and you can already see that it's making a difference to your life. So why would you want to go back to those old, destructive habits? Sticking to your Self-Confidence Protection Plan is the best way to make this feeling last, but the truth is, you can never completely avoid setbacks. You can't predict the future, and there's a good chance that something unexpected will test your new conviction. If you keep your good habits going, you'll weather the storm. Remember, every challenge to your self-confidence is a chance to learn about you, about how you relate to other people, and about how the world works. You can't put a price on knowledge like that!

Life Lesson

If you take just one thing from this book, it should be this – thoughts are just thoughts. What does that mean? It means that just because you think something, even if you believe it very strongly, it doesn't follow that it's true. Some thoughts are just plain wrong, and some are no more than habits. Your thoughts are not you, and they're not necessarily accurate or helpful, either. Changing the way you think really can change your experience of life. With practice and commitment, you can adjust your perspective on yourself so that your thoughts and actions towards yourself are compassionate, helpful, productive and supportive, rather than sabotaging you and holding you back. The end result is self-confidence – the ability to accept and appreciate yourself, just as you are.

OTHER THINGS THAT MIGHT HELP

I hope you've found this book helpful. You may also find the following books and organisations of interest or further help.

Books

Beck, Aaron T., *Love is Never Enough*, New York: Penguin Books, 1989

Burns, David D., *The Feeling Good Handbook*, New York: Plume/Penguin Books, 1990

Butler, Gillian, *Overcoming Social Anxiety and Shyness*, London: Robinson, 1999

Gilbert, Paul, *Overcoming Depression*, London: Robinson, 2009 (3rd edition)

Greenberger, Dennis and Padesky, Christine A., *Mind Over Mood: A Cognitive Therapy Treatment Manual for Clients*, New York: Guilford, 1995

McKay, Matthew and Fanning, Patrick, *Self-Esteem*, Oakland, California: New Harbinger Publications 1992 (2nd edition)

Organisations

British Association of Behavioural and Cognitive
Psychotherapies (BABCP)
Imperial House
Hornby Street
BURY
BL9 5BN
Tel: 0161 705 5bn
Email: babcp@babcp.com
Website: www.babcp.com

Professional organisation for CBT therapists. Has a
database of accredited CBT therapists which you can
search to find a suitable therapist close to where you
live or work.

British Association for Counselling and Psychotherapy
(BACP)
BACP House
15 St John's Business Park
Lutterworth
LE17 4HB,
Tel: 01455 883300
Minicom: 01455 550307; Text: 01455 560606
Website: www.bacp.co.uk

Professional organisation for a large number of
different kinds of counselling and psychotherapies.
Has a database of counsellors and psychotherapists
in the UK.

Mind: The National Association for Mental Health
15-19 Broadway
Stratford
London
E15 4BQ

Mind Cymru
3rd Floor
Quebec House
Castlebridge
5-19 Cowbridge Road East
Cardiff
CF11 9AB
Mind InfoLine: 0845 766 0163
Email: contact@mind.org.uk
Website: www.mind.org.uk

Leading mental health charity for England and Wales.
Provides information and advice on mental health issues
and campaigns on behalf of those experiencing mental
distress.

INDEX

Note: the following abbreviations have been used:
t – table; *f* – figure